Once Upon a Dime

# Once Upon a Dime

## Heaven is Talking to Us. Do You Know How to Listen?

Monica L Morrissey

Monica L. Morrissey LLC

# CONTENTS

CONTENTS

# Reader Reviews

**What readers are saying about *Once Upon a Dime***

*Once Upon a Dime by Monica Morrissey was a beautiful, moving and evidential (of an afterlife) story.*

*This is a sequel to her first book on the topic, Dimes from Heaven, with of which share how and why dimes became a sign from her dad after he passed away. Monica not only shares some pretty mind-blowing times she got dimes, how other people got dimes (or other signs), but also helps guide us how to notice signs and communications from our discarnates (what I refer to as our loved ones who have passed away). She has some interactions with other people with some unexpected twists that are a little hard to dismiss as coincidence.*

*Monica also openheartedly shares about grief, loss and learning to be honest with our emotions and that all of our relationships with those who we love are not perfect - they can be far from it, but we love them anyway. She is very open about herself, her loved ones, who she is and her life's ups and downs in a brave and relatable way. Whatever you think about an afterlife, you will come away from reading this thinking that these are some remarkable "signs" that are hard to just dismiss.*

Liz Entin: Entrepreneur, Author of WTF Just Happened?!: A sciencey-skeptic explores grief, healing, and evidence of and afterlife, Podcast Host: WTF Just Happened?!: All about the afterlife. No woo. www.wtfjusthappened.net

PS
*I want you to know the following - I've been planning and saving today to finish the write up. Sorry to be a little behind. But...*
*1 - I never use cash. Ever.*
*2 - I never take coins on the VERY rare occasion I use cash*
*3 - I went to sweep my floor and clean a bit before getting to work so place is comfy*
*And.... I found A DIME!!!!*
*4 - also note bc I'm sciencey I asked as an experiment to get a dime in some way when I finish the book - I didn't think I would! In fact I forgot I had even asked over a week ago."*

### Darcey Elizabeth
*"Losing my mom at the age of 29, I found myself angry because I had so much left to say to her. I always kept thinking, if only I could tell her this one last thing. Then I got the privilege to read, **"Once Upon a Dime"** by the amazing Monica Morrissey. This book helped me realize that I can talk to her and the signs I received confirmed just that.*

*The sign from my mom is a Cardinal. Before my mom passed, she gave me a little cardinal luck charm with a prayer to hold on to for my speaking events. I used to be deathly afraid of public speaking. While reading "**Once Upon a Dime**", I noticed that anytime I have a moment of question, a Cardinal comes to my window. Then I noticed I started to see them everywhere from tablecloths to pictures to the outside.*

*Receiving signs from Heaven can be powerful and has changed my life. In this book, Monica provides insightful guidance on the process of recognizing and interpreting these signs. Drawing on both personal experiences and expert knowledge, Monica offers practical exercises to help readers develop their intuition and cultivate a deeper connection. Whether you're seeking comfort, guidance, or looking for confirmation, this book is a must-read, highly recommended!"*

*Darcey Elizabeth, Founder of Claim Your Network, Podcast host and entrepeneur, www.claimyournetwork.com*

# Foreword

You are about to be connected to the Heavens above through your own human experiences. If you were looking for a way to move forward on your soul light journey, then you have the right book in your hands. My name is Rebecca Anne LoCicero, and I am right beside you on this adventure. I have always been aligned to spirit and have joyfully and willingly been bringing everyone I know toward those connections. This book guides you and connects you naturally by the words of the author. A gift, this book is the forward motion we all need to get that feeling of *really receiving* a gift from our loved ones in Heaven.

I have been working as a psychic medium in the public eye since 1994. I have been able to travel and present my trademark presentation Messages from HeavenTM to many audiences. These galleries are part of my work. I love to bring the reality that Heaven is real to as many people as I can. I do that by bringing through validating and accurate messages directly from the true personality of the loved one's soul they have lost. I do tend to be a bit brassy; it comes with the confidence I have in the truths in the messages they share with me. Once such gallery in Vermont happens to have had a woman right up front and I had to ask her if that was "a f'n dime she was wearing on her necklace', which at the time was a sign through me for her that she was getting a hello' from her dad in spirit. Little did I know then that her dime would become my dime too, and now, your dime as well.

I have been connected to Monica Morrissey, your author, since that first group. I was overjoyed when she presented her first book, *Dimes from Heaven,* where she clearly embraced all the empathic energy that was already within her. I have seen many people enter the metaphysical realms and find themselves seeking teachers whilst becoming one themselves. Monica has now found herself on this journey. I have seen her start to present at seminars and conventions as she put her second book out, *More Dimes from Heaven.*

*Once Upon a Dime....* leaves you with an endless amount of amazing resources to continue your learning and expanding into your own 'Conquest for Dimes'. This third book takes you through the feelings of grief balanced by the stories of survival. You'll feel the pain of finding and losing signs while you gain the confidence to clearly ask for more signs. As a medium, I find that the most important part of living without your loved ones is to clearly see the signs as a hello and an 'I love you' from those we are missing. If you can find a way to bring yourself a touch of the peace they feel in Heaven, you can feel a calmness within that grieving process. As human beings, we need that. Monica expands the basics of grief steps while allowing you to accept your human emotions. Moving forward, this book allows you to believe in miracles. You'll feel as if you are walking with her and taking deep breaths alongside her as she climbs mountains to find signs. You'll see how a sign from your loved one can be more than just a 'hello', it can be a full-on validation of a moment in your life! Through a barrage of characters, family and friends of Monica's you are able to vicariously relate to each encounter. Let her change your perceptions, choose love, meet your light body.
By Psychic Medium/Author, Rebecca Anne LoCicero
www.RebeccaAnneLoCicero.com
May 2023

**Once Upon a Dime**

Once upon a time, there was a woman who was showered with dimes.

She knew these dimes were the keys to connect each time.

When she was a little girl,

She knew there was more to life than the eyes could see,

More than the ears could hear,

More than the nose could smell,

Most of all she knew that she was connected to something in her heart.

She didn't have the words to explain it to others.

She didn't have the knowledge she needed yet to connect to this place.

She knew that what she was feeling was so real.

She went on with her life but seemed lost.

She tried to fit in to what society seemed to communicate to her.

She was told to keep reaching for more.

That was the only way to happiness.

The search seemed like a never ending to do list.

She was told that fear was more real than love.


One dime at a time, they guided her back home.

Heaven is near, not far.

Heaven is a feeling, not a place.

Heaven is all around us, not above us.

Heaven is a way to be, not a place to go.

Heaven is right here right now.


Supported, alive, guided,
she now

Smelled the memories.

Saw the lights.

Heard the guidance.

Felt the love from within.


No longer lost, she began a new relationship with life,

She now knew the roses she smelled,

Were her Grandmother nearby.

She now knew the lights flickering were her guardian angels.

She felt the messages in her heart and

Knew the garden of life was the key to happiness.

She listened to the messages from the Divine,

With each found Dime.


She felt connected to this mystical, invisible dimension that she knew as a child.

Most of all, her heart felt the love she had longed for.

No longer chasing happiness, she was able to live life in gratitude.

No longer living in fear, she knew love was all that was needed.

Each dime was filled with unending love,

Connecting our souls forever.


**Thank you, Dad, for the Dimes from Heaven**

# 1

## My First Dimes

*"So many different synchronicities have taken place in my life over the last few years that confirm for me again and again how connected we actually are. For me, a synchronicity is when a connection is made between myself and someone else that is so utterly beyond chance, so stunningly transparent and unlikely, that the idea of a simple coincidence is way too far-fetched even to consider."*
*~Anita Moorjani*

Tears flowed freely down my cheeks with each step I took. My eyes burned, making it challenging to see. This had to be one of the hardest hikes I had ever done. The trail up the mountain was easy and it was a warm sunny day. I was out of breath but that wasn't why the hike was difficult. The difficulty was in my mind, and I could not imagine the intense pain I would feel when I reached the top of the mountain. Each step up the gravelly path brought more stabbing pain to my heart. As I came upon the steep moss-covered rocks and saw the white birch trees, I was getting closer to my favorite spot to call my dad. My friend, Peggy, had told me, "You will know what to do when you get there."

Questions spun in my mind like a fast-moving merry-go-round. How would I know what to do? What did she mean? How would I ever get through this? As I sat on the bumpy rock and looked out to see the sun forming diamonds on the lake, I remembered the last time I called my father from this very spot. Our family camp, a rustic, modified 1930's cabin with wood paneling, sat at the northeastern point on the lake below. It was partially covered by a tree, but that didn't matter. I knew exactly where it was. When I called my dad, he would be sitting inside the living room as he peered out the cathedral ceiling windows toward the mountain when he said, "Can you see us waving?"

Growing up in the 70's, who would have thought that a person would be able to call another person from on top of a mountain? When I was young, the phone was always connected to the wall. Heck, when my family purchased our first cordless phone, it was like we had won the lottery. How would anyone in the 80's ever believe that voices would be able to travel through time and space through a little black box? My understanding of the possibilities of communication was only just beginning.

I would laugh and say, "Yes! I can see you," even though it was too far to see anyone from on top of a mountain even if peering through a set of binoculars. It would be like looking at ants while on top of a hundred foot ladder.

grief, I wondered if it might just be possible to connect one last time. I had no idea how to do this and no idea if it would be able to happen. Can we really communicate to people who no longer have a physical body? And, can they really send us messages? Could I believe in something that I couldn't see and might not be able to prove? Could it be possible for this invisible communication system to work like a cell phone- traveling through time and space with no wires or anything physical to connect us?

Shortly before his death, I had explained to my father what I believed to be true. Illness had taken over his body and his eyes were closed, but I was hopeful that he heard me say, "Hey Dad, there is this new communication system you haven't heard about yet. It's where people who don't have a body anymore are able to talk to people still on earth. You won't really be away from us. We are able to talk all the time because your soul is in spirit form and is always here with us. We are always connected."

My father might have thought I was telling a fairytale bedtime story like he might have done when I was a little girl. Hours later, his soul left his body and went to the spirit world. If my father was able to whisper to me, I think he would have given me the key to understanding death. He would have told me, "The end is not the end. Be aware and not only will you be able to hear me, but I'll send you physical signs that show I am near." This is what happens when people arrive in Heaven and I now know that he understood this.

Trembling, my eyes still stinging from the tears, I sat on the rock and looked out over the rolling hills and lush green mountains of Vermont. My body was tense with grief and pain at the thought of never seeing or talking with my dad again.

I suddenly realized there were two couples behind me now, exploring the cement foundation of the old wooden cabin that burned years ago. I quickly wiped my tears and tried to pull myself together.

I began explaining my disheveled state to them. "I'm sorry, I must look like a wreck. My father died last week. I always used to call him when I got to this particular spot on the mountain."

The older woman responded, "I'm so sorry. Would it be alright with you if we gave you a hug?"

I was dripping in sweat and tears and I'm sure my aroma wasn't the sweetest, but these people didn't seem to mind. I kept talking and one by one, I received hugs from each and every one of those strangers on top of that mountain.

"My family has a camp on that side of the lake. Growing up, I spent every summer there. Even my great grandparents owned the Elmore Store on the other end of the lake," I explained, wondering why I felt the need to keep talking to these people. I could just walk away and go back down the mountain. I could stay in my own little world, filled with grief and despair. I didn't. I chose to connect with these people.

"Wow, that is so neat," I can't remember who said it but they responded politely and looked where I pointed. "This is such a beautiful spot."

"I'm so sorry. I feel like I am ruining your hike with my sadness," I apologized again.

The younger gentleman walked over closer to me, looked deep into my eyes and asked, "Do you have faith?"

Tears ran down my cheeks like fast dripping raindrops and my body shook more as I grasped the dime on my necklace between my thumb and forefinger. A few months ago, my father had given me a 1919 Liberty head dime from his antique coin collection. That dime reminded me of my father, but I felt the special powers infusing my heart with love and faith.

Faith and love for me are like the wind blowing; they are all invisible but you know the wind is there when it cools your skin. Faith blows goosebumps on me reminding me that there is an invisible force of life, an energy in the air that one senses without physical proof. All are invisible but powerful. Was this invisible connection really possible? Could our thoughts travel through time and space like a cell phone? The communication is between souls- even without a physical body. Is there some sort of soul consciousness that continues after death?

I had shared with my dad how much the dime meant to me.

"Do you know how special those dimes are that you gave to all of us kids?" I asked him. We were riding in his light blue mini van heading back from his camp on the lake to his home just ten minutes away. As we drove down the hill toward town, I said "A dime is just a dime unless it is a dime from your father. Then it is a *dime*!" This would be my dad's last car ride and one of our last conversations.

He didn't respond but looked down as he shook his head in agreement. His cough seemed to increase the flow of tears. His body seemed to be betraying his will to live and at seventy-nine, heart disease was taking over his physical body. He was scared; not knowing what the next part of his soul journey would be like.

"Yes, my faith is very strong," I replied and smiled at this man who dared to ask me such a personal question. His next words would surprise me even more as my tears changed to happy, joyful tears. I was still shaking and crying, but it was different. I was filled with love even with my broken heart.

"I am a minister. Would you like to say a prayer from your father?" he asked me.

Could this minister on the mountain really be the phone call from my father that I had requested? Could this coincidence really be the communication that other people talk about and I thought might only be a silly fantasy?

As I stood face to face, holding sweaty hands with a stranger on top of my favorite mountain, I knew my father was somehow able to arrange this to prove to me that the invisible spirit communication system worked. He was able to call me without wires or cell service, just like I had explained to him. Death did not end our relationship. His soul traveled on without his physical body and his energy form was now near. A new relationship with my father was beginning to develop; one that was very different than when my father was here on earth. My father was able to show me unconditional love from where his soul lived on.

The next week I hiked the mountain again. It didn't seem quite as difficult as the week before. I was out of breath again but there were no tears. Some say time heals grief but I'm not sure it really does. Mostly, time changes my grief and as life moved on, I felt more at peace. I was at peace on this hike because I truly felt that my father had "called" me, exactly one week ago.

"Hey Merrilee, I'm on top of the mountain. Remember when you and dad used to pretend to wave to me?" I laughed into my cell phone as I paced near that same rock. I couldn't sit down this time. I was all alone and the fall air cooled my sweaty skin, sending shivers through my entire body.

Merrilee was there each and every day to care for my father during his last summer on the lake. She laughed as she corrected me,

"We weren't pretending! We were actually waving to you. Your father and I would laugh and say, 'Do you think she can see us?'"

I laughed, imagining the fun Merrilee brought to my Dad's life. "I sure do miss his sense of humor."

"Me too. I am so happy that I got to know him. He was such a good, kind man." As I walked and talked with Merrilee, I gazed into the horizon filled with trees beginning their transformation from green to a splattering of yellow, red and orange. I wondered about my father and what it was like for him now, after his transition to spirit form. My imagination seemed to be running wild as I felt like my dad was right there with me.

I wasn't looking at my immediate surroundings, but I knew the wild rose bushes were on the far side of the clearing and the pine trees were behind me. They were as familiar to me as my own home. As I walked and talked, I remembered to look down so I wouldn't trip on the uneven ground near the rock.

When I looked down, I couldn't believe what my eyes saw in the dirt right near the tip of my hiking boot.

I gasped into the phone. "Oh my gosh, Merrilee. You are never going to believe what I just found." As my mind wondered about the reality of this, I moved as if in slow motion bending down to pick it up.

"I don't know. What is it?" her curiosity peaked by my comment about finding something on top of a mountain. A moment in time to share with another person is what makes memories in our hearts. This one is forever with me.

It glistened in the sunshine showing me the invisible communication system was working yet again. I felt like the princess in the story and my prince sent me the love that filled my broken heart. Smiling from ear to ear I exclaimed, "A dime! Merrilee, there is a dime right here in the dirt!"

How could this be? How does a coin, this particular coin, land on top of the mountain exactly in this spot? Was my father grinning like this was some sort of game to him? Could he really do things like this without his physical body? It was a sign that could only mean one thing. For the second week in a row, he was sending me a message that even in his death he was always with me.

Time stopped as Merrilee and I processed the chances of me finding a dime on the top of a mountain exactly in this spot.

"I can't believe it. How could that happen? Do you think your father did this? I have goosebumps!" Merrilee talked as I looked at the coin.

"The year on the dime is 1995 and there is a P just above the year," I told her.

"What year was your son, Patrick, born?"

My smile grew as big as an upside-down rainbow. "1995."

We laughed and the tears squirted onto my cheeks. They were the same happy tears when the minister asked if I had faith. My whole body was alive with energy, electrical currents running through my blood. Even though it had been a few short weeks since my father's death, suddenly this coincidence helped me transform my intense grief into pure love and happiness. My immense gratitude for this moment was difficult to explain as love poured into my heart like a full cup of red wine.

My father's sideways grin and the twinkle in his eye revealed to me that he still had his sense of humor. His voice was clear in my head when he said, "Yes! It is me! I figured out that spirit communication system. Isn't it great? We really can connect from here. You told me my 'engine' would still be running, this engine is so different! I'm not in any pain and my engine will run forever!"

I had no idea that this first dime would lead me to write three books! Pennies seemed to pop out of the concrete wherever I walked ever since my mother died. When she was alive, she would have rolled her eyes at me while explaining, "When you are dead, you're dead. It's the end."

I didn't want to believe that and these events gave me the verification to believe our souls are like a car engine that never stops. Our physical body was just the frame of the car that the engine traveled in during our earthly life. The engine traveled on and through many coincidences and synchronicities, my father's and my mother's engines were alive and well. And, the invisible communication system worked as slick as calling from a cell phone. We didn't need wires. We needed faith to believe that our loved ones' souls are right here with us - mostly invisible to the naked eye, but palpable in our heart.

The dime on the mountain wouldn't prompt me to write my first book, *Dimes From Heaven*. It would be two years later and another coincidence.

Anxiety about my son purchasing a new house at the age of twenty-two consumed my thoughts. As I helped clean the entire kitchen, scrubbing the black moldy grime hiding under the fridge, I wondered if this was the right decision for him.

Dog and cat hair seemed to cling to every part of the house. As I vacuumed the bedroom, a penny ricocheted off the baseboard heater near the wall. I smiled as I thought of my mom. As I crawled into the bedroom closet to vacuum up all of the accumulated pet hair, a dime popped out of the closet door jamb. I smiled as I felt a deep connection to my dad.

Our Realtor, who was a good friend of ours, had predicted that we would find a dime and she was right! Since my friends had heard my story about the dime on the mountain, I posted a picture of the dime on Facebook. I felt as if my parents were here with my son in his new home.

That wasn't why I ran out of the house screaming like I was announcing a fire to my son and husband who were up on the roof checking out the broken chimney. Instead of a warning, I was confirming my belief that I received another clear message from my father.

"You cannot call me crazy anymore!" Of course, they had no idea what I was holding in my hand or how strongly I believed that this coincidence was a form of communication from what I call the "other side"- where our souls live after they leave the physical body.

The filthy green rug in the small spare bedroom was so dirty that it was going to need to be either shampooed or replaced.

I was dead tired. We had been cleaning all day. At the last minute, I spotted a nickel caught in between the wires that were shooting through the wooden floorboards. Something urged me to get that coin. I sort of almost freaked out when I thought the vacuum almost ate it up. I wish I had the fingers the size of a two year old as I could barely squeeze my thumb and forefinger into the hole trying to grab the edge of it. My fingers slipped. I felt I was playing a game of tug of war. Who would win? And why did I feel like I needed to get this nickel? I mean, it was only worth five cents!

It wasn't a nickel.

It was a 1936 Liberty head dime; the exact type of dime that I wore in my necklace from my father. My anxiety disappeared as quickly as a bubble could pop. My son was meant to buy this house and my father gave his approval with that special dime. This coincidence didn't seem random. It felt like a magical dime confirming again this invisible connection to my father.

I could tell dime stories all day long. When we believe in this mysterious connection to the Spirit world, it seems to activate the communication system even more. I wrote my first book, *Dimes From Heaven,* to share my inspiring dime story and help people believe in signs from our loved ones. I had no idea that sharing my story would create a series of events that were too incredible not to share!

For example, when I went to pick up my business cards, the store employees asked me about my book. Then, to my surprise, they shared they had a dime glued to their floor as a joke on an employee! Can you believe it? The business I decided to use to print my business cars has a dime glued to the floor of their building! What are the chances? Then, on the day my second book, *More Dimes From Heaven,* was published, a dime literally popped out of the grass as I raked my lawn. I said to my husband, "Can you believe this?" As he shook his head and smiled, he responded with a simple, "Yes, of course. It always happens just when you need it." Even though I now understand how this all works, I am still surprised when coincidences happen!

I didn't always believe that our souls traveled on after death. In fact, I took life for granted most of the time and thought most people would be able to live into their seventies, eighties, or even nineties. It wasn't until I experienced the shocking death of a loved one that I began to wonder not only about death but about life as well.

Ever since I was young, I wondered about death. I had not grown up with this knowledge or belief system and I was curious as to whether or not it was really possible to connect with our loved ones who were gone. They say that when the student is ready, the teacher shall appear. Even though my job at the time was as a public school teacher, I was a student learning about life and death in a whole new way.

What happens when we die? Why do young people have to die? How does a parent go on living after the death of a child? Are mediums real? Can a butterfly really be a sign from someone's mother? Where do our souls go when they leave the physical body? What would happen to me if something happened to my child? What would my children do if something happened to me?

I had a few friends who thought that butterflies were messages but I often doubted it. I mean, really? How many butterflies do I see every summer? How could that possibly be a sign? The thing about signs from Heaven is that a person might not believe until something happens to them that is so crazy, like my dime on the mountain or in my son's house, that the coincidences convince them that it must be true.

On April 24, 2008, the fast track education about life after death began for me.

"Tyler was in an accident," my sister-in-law told me as I held the cordless landline to my ear. When she called me on April 25th, I imagined a minor accident for my twenty-one-year-old nephew. Maybe his car hit a tree or went into the ditch. My kids were only twelve and fourteen at the time which meant I had no idea what it was like to have a child who could drive.

"He's okay. Banged up and in the hospital but he will be fine." These are the words I imagined her saying next. They are the words I didn't hear.

Her voice was difficult to understand but in between her sobs she explained, "He's gone. He died."

Speechless, I handed the phone to my husband, who was glaring at me, as if he already knew something was seriously wrong. The fear was in the air and my children sensed it. You could almost smell the shock like a gas leak warning us of danger. Except, the shocking news of death wasn't a smell; it was an invisible feeling radiating from our bodies.

In moments like this, our hearts beat faster and time slows down. It's probably the same feeling that I felt as a baby inside my mother's womb when she received the shocking news that her father died suddenly of a heart attack. It was just a few short weeks before I was born. My soul knows about losing a loved one quickly and unexpectedly. The adrenaline that traveled like a river in her blood would travel in my blood too. It wasn't a feeling in the air like the phone call; it was an emotion traveling in the blood we shared. My DNA footprint was established and as a soul not even born yet, I forever would be affected by the sudden death of my mother's father.

My children experienced the unforeseen grief of losing one of their beloved cousins and how they managed it would depend on how I handled the news. This would be a hard lesson for me to learn as a mother, and I didn't feel ready. I could barely keep myself together as tears sprang into my eyes and dribbled down my cheeks. Soon, the water spigot would open up on their cheeks too. And, at this time, I had no knowledge of there even being a possibility to be able to connect with someone after they were gone.

Tyler died immediately on impact when the car, driven by a friend of his, hit a large brick mailbox in Tennessee. Tyler's death forever sent me searching for answers to questions I had never discussed with anyone.

Grief is so different when it is a young person or a sudden death. This was many years before my parents died and this sudden shock to our family was the first time my children experienced such a deep, transformative loss. As a mother, I wanted my children to be able to talk about their cousin who they missed dearly and I wanted them to appreciate how precious life really is.

Our family talked about Tyler and anytime the number eight appeared, we thought of him.

We began to feel the energy of Tyler thanks to his best friend, David Price. David knew that Tyler was with him when he pitched his first game on a major league baseball field.

"No one enjoyed David Price's performance in Tuesday night's All-Star Game as much as Tyler Morrissey did. He was in the upper deck. He was behind the dugout. He was behind the plate. He was even on the mound with Price. After all, as far as Price is concerned, he always is. Almost three months after Tyler's death, David felt Tyler's presence- helping David as he began his MLB career as a pitcher. This was something that Tyler always believed would happen to David and David knew that Tyler's spirit was right there with him every step of the way."

~Gary Shelton St. Petersburg Time July 13, 2010

Our family loves to watch David pitch. Do you ever notice how he looks up? Or taps his heart? If David believed, could we also believe Tyler was still here with us? Would I be able to guide my children to believe in something different than how I was raised?

I went searching for answers about the afterlife and what I found surprised me. A friend recommended I read Brian Weiss's book, *Many Lives Many Masters.* Brian was a psychiatrist and a skeptic about anything that science couldn't prove or anything we couldn't sense with our five human senses. After losing his son as a baby, he had no intention of understanding anything about the after life. Death changes our lives in ways we may never have imagined. During hypnosis, one of Brian's psychiatric patients remembered many past lives. One life she shared was when she was killed. She knew the name of the person and other facts about the person's life. She had no way of knowing the information she spoke about during the hypnosis but Brian was able to verify every piece of information she said during the sessions. He went on to write about how souls return to earth to experience many lifetimes and how important it is to turn to love instead of fear.

In my research, I discovered that our soul, which is the spiritual part of our physical body, chooses our life plan to learn and grow. We choose the best time for our growth to come to earth to learn the lessons we need to learn as we are each on a different path. Each event in our life has something to teach us. Some souls stay for a short time and others stay longer. Tyler's time here wasn't nearly long enough.

I helped care for my father-in-law during the last few days of his life. His death wasn't a shock as he lived eighty-eight wonderful years. He had seven beautiful children and a wife of sixty-three years whom he loved dearly. Even in the last few days while confined to his bed, he cherished his bride.

His transition brought back so many memories of my own father. Each day, as we navigated the Hospice care, we were reminded of how heart disease slowly takes over until there is no life left.

My in-laws' faith carried us through the week, accepting that Jack would be with God soon. We knew his time was near. Since I was at the house around the clock to help the family care for him, the chances of me finding a dime were slim.

I found a penny on the bathroom floor one morning. It hadn't been there all week and then all of a sudden, there it was! My mom was sending love to me and my husband's family.

I placed the penny in the pocket of my shorts. I was reading in the formal living room while the family spent time in the small den where their father's hospital bed crowded the small space. Later that day, I reached into my pocket and the penny was gone. I retraced my steps back to the blue armchair. As I sat down, and pushed the cushion to the side just a bit, I found the penny.

In the exact spot where the penny was, there was a dime right next to it. Can you believe it? The penny led me to the dime, almost like the universe creating a scavenger hunt! I felt both my mom and dad were with me helping us say goodbye to Jack. They would soon be welcoming Jack to the spirit world.

A few hours later, my dear father-in-law transitioned. I imagined my father telling Jack all about the spirit communication system and I'm sure they both will send some more dimes. (While working on this chapter, my niece, Madeleine and Mother-in-law found two dimes! 7/27/21)

Jack passed away quietly in his home with his bride holding his hand. This loss wasn't like the experience the family had years ago when my nephew died at the young age of twenty-one. It doesn't matter how our loved ones transition to the spirit world, they want to connect with us. They are right there waiting for us to ask and to have faith that it works!

Some people are uncomfortable talking about death, regardless of whether it is their own death or the death of someone else. When I was growing up we most definitely weren't encouraged to talk about any kind of "weird" signs from people who were gone.

I grew up thinking that "those" type of people were a bit on the crazy side. After Tyler's death, a few of my close friends wanted to go see a medium. We weren't really sure about it and wondered if they could really receive messages from dead people. Over the years, I slowly reframed my beliefs about the possibility of an after life- one where our souls are somehow still intact, even though our bodies are gone. It wasn't until both of my parents died that I was able to put into practice everything I had learned about the spirit world.

I never intended to be a writer but felt that my dime stories might help others experiencing grief. I was surprised by the number of people, even in my small town in Vermont, who believed in signs from those who had passed. I guess that before I shared my story, people might not have talked about signs from dead people because people might think they were a bit on the crazy side. Nowadays, it seems so much more acceptable than it did years ago. The more people reached out to me, the more stories that seemed to unfold in my life made me realize that we don't need to be a medium to be able to connect to the spirit world. We are born with this ability. We just need to know how to access it.

These days, I am one of "those" people my mother would have brushed off as nonsense. She understands now because when a soul transforms back to the spirit world, there is an immediate understanding about their soul lessons. They leave behind all other human emotions because in the Spirit world there is only love and light. My mother even showed me her approval and love when I published my first book. (keep reading- you'll find out about this story in chapter three!)

We all experience grief in a different way. Within the sadness, there is also a certain amount of love in our hearts when we know that our souls continue on and are able to communicate. We are all connected and there is another dimension to this life to explore.

The more that I wrote about these coincidences, the more synchronicities happened to me and those around me. These experiences altered my life, enlightening me to live in a more spiritual way.

Something happens when we decide to share these stories about how people communicate in the after-life. Other people "catch" the signs, just like a cold is contagious. People start finding dimes or coincidences happen where people stop and wonder, "Could this really be true?"

Story by story the evidence and the strategies help to understand:

- The possibilities of an after-life
- Popular signs from Heaven
- That coincidences and synchronicities have meaning
- How to request and receive a sign from your loved one

- How understanding death helps us to be grateful for the life we have been given
- How to listen to your intuition using your natural born spiritual abilities

Since ancient times, cultures around the world have told stories. Our brains love the full circle loop that comes from a story. Each story is filled with deep pain and sorrow for the ones we miss but also filled with love when the key opens the door to the communication system.

Chapter by chapter the stories about communication from what I call "the other side," in which souls who have passed on are free to visit in energy form may transform some of your pain so you feel unending love. Somehow our loved ones create coincidences that can only mean one thing, "The end is not the end." Like a cell phone with no wires, our souls are forever connected with unending love. These incredible stories empower you to use intentional thoughts to connect with your loved ones in the Spirit world and learn to live in a more spiritual way, where the things we cannot see inspire us all.

# 2

## Experiencing Grief- Beyond the Five Stages

"Sometimes I forget how rich I am. My hot water works on a dime, my a/c works when I need it to. I can go to any grocery store and purchase what I please to eat. I have a clean kitchen to cook in. I have a clean shower to bathe in...sometimes I forget I'm beyond blessed." ~Author unknown

If there is one thing in life people can be sure of is that they are going to die. Eventually, the body we were given at birth will fade away and many will wonder, "Does this mean I am gone forever?" I've wondered about why I am here on earth for so long that now I don't know what it would be like to not wonder about my life.

When I was growing up and a person died, the person was erased like hitting the delete button on a computer. They were gone and there was nothing else to discuss. We did not celebrate their life and we didn't even express how sad we were that they were gone. My family didn't discuss death before it happened and we definitely didn't talk about the possibility of someone else dying. I barely heard stories about my Grandfather who died two weeks before my birth.

The most well-known stages of grief in America were developed by Kubler Ross in 1969 (I was one year old!) and these would become so ingrained into our society that fifty years later they are still accepted (in America) as the only way to grieve. Some are guided to "heal" by "moving through" the stages. Why are we using such an outdated system? I'm not still using the telephone system from the sixties, why would I use an outdated psychological process for dealing with a major life event?

What most people might not know is that Kubler-Ross and David Kessler designed the five stages to be used for people who were facing their own death. They didn't create them to use after a person died.

The five stages developed by Kubler-Ross & Kessler are the following: 1. denial 2. anger 3. bargaining 4. depression 5. acceptance. A person who lost a loved one is made to feel that if you dealt with these feelings, eventually you would feel better. As anyone who has experienced the deep loss of their loved ones knows, grief is not something that goes away. Losing someone affects us for the rest of our lives.

I remember when my mother died. I definitely wasn't in (1)denial-she was gone. How could I deny that? I was (2)angry. I was angry that she wouldn't go get help when she knew she was sick. How was anger going to help me feel better? It wouldn't bring her back so it was pointless to be angry. (3)Bargaining? What was I to bargain for? She was gone and there was nothing to do but live without her. The (4)depression didn't catch up to me for years after her death. My father most definitely experienced depression and wondered why he was left behind. He was ready to go be with her. My depression hit later on when I realized that I never had the relationship with my mother that I wanted. (5)Acceptance seemed to be difficult at first but with time, there was nothing else to do but create a new life without my mother.

David Kessler added two new stages to the five stages - shock and finding meaning. The shock felt by an unexpected death can rock us to our core. When this happens to me I feel like time stops and nothing else in life matters anymore. It's like I'm watching a movie and I am one of the characters. I get angry easily and can't seem to focus on anything. Nothing else seems important. After the initial paralyzed feeling, then it's time to create a new way to live without the physical presence of the person.

It is difficult to describe but there is this overwhelming, unbearable feeling, especially if the death is a surprise. Brene Brown nails the emotion in her new book, *Atlas of the Heart*. She calls it anguish and this is her description," Anguish is an almost unbearable and traumatic swirl of shock, incredulity, grief, and powerlessness." It feels like life is so out of my control that there is no way to get through the experience. Since we all do get through it, I wonder what the lasting effects are of those moments when we first learn about a death. The trauma stays in our bones and radiates within our bodies. It's what I felt as a baby inside my mother's womb, but as a child I didn't have the resources to process the grief.

One thing that I believe is missing from the stages is anxiety. When someone dies, I immediately think, "Oh no, what if I die? What if someone close to me dies?" I go to this place where everything is scary. What if I have cancer? What if I have heart disease? What if someone I love gets into a car accident? Everyday becomes scarier and scarier. I have to remind myself that each day is not promised. I have to remind myself of the value in being alive and that our time on earth is determined by a greater power than me. I am able to take steps to create a healthy life but, ultimately, when it is time to go, we all leave this earth and transition back to our spirit form.

What if there was another way to experience grief? What if there weren't linear stages to work through like we were attending school and trying to graduate? What if through our loss we found strength and a deep connection to something beyond human explanation- like universal spirit or our own soul? What if we allowed our grief to express itself every single time it appeared? And then, we took time to remember the love of the person who was gone. What if we found meaning through the experience or decided to find meaning in our loved ones' life? And decided to embrace that part of them in our own life?

I've noticed a difference in how people experience death depending on their belief in God. When I speak of God, I'm not talking necessarily about a specific religion or a man up in the sky controlling everything. What I mean is there is a universal, invisible connection to "something" and that "something" is "out there" and "in here". "Out there" includes many mysteries like nature, the solar system and all of life. How else are we able to explain how a tree grows or how animals live or how the moon circles the earth? The "in here" is a feeling within us that feels love and connection. Our hearts are alive and connected to "something". This connection with God or universal intelligence or whatever we want to call it is so much more than we are able to put into words and it requires trust; which I call faith. If we allow this connection to "something", then our life experiences are filled with awe and wonder.

There are two other models of grief that may help more than the original stages. J. William Worden's four tasks of grieving (from his book *Grief Counseling and Grief Therapy)* and Thomas Attig's grief process (from his book *How We Grieve: Relearning the World)* introduce us to a different perspective.

Worden's tasks are not linear in fashion and may be done for the rest of your life. There is no graduation in your grief and it is acceptable to continue your journey using these. The four tasks are 1. Accept the Reality of the Loss 2. Process Your Grief and Pain 3. Adjust to the World Without Your Loved One 4. Find a Way to Maintain a Connection to Your Loved One. These tasks allow for a lot of emotions during the process. And, personally speaking, I love number four as that is what has helped me the most. Grief and death have changed my life in such incredible ways that I never would have imagined.

Thomas Attig's process includes some of the similar tasks to Worden's. Thomas suggests the following: 1. Changes in the Physical World 2. Changes in Relationships with Others Still Living 3. Changes in Perspective on Time 4. Changes in Spiritual Grounding 5. Changes in Relationship with the Deceased 6. Changes in Identity.

Both of these models allow you to stay connected to your loved one. This is the key to experiencing life after loss. Without this connection, the pain and suffering can be overwhelming. As David Kessler states in his book, *Finding Meaning*, "Pain is inevitable. Suffering is optional." David also wrote, "When we move through pain and we release it, we fear there will be nothing, but the truth is, when the pain is gone, we are connected only in love."

Recently, I was chatting with a co-worker who found meaning in her friend's death. Tracy shared with me that her lifetime friend, Missy, passed away due to cancer and because of this, Tracy had a whole new outlook on life. Tracy said that the family was not having a "funeral" but they were going to have a Celebration of Life instead. She explained that Missy was full of life and that, along with their tears, they were going to remember all the great things about Missy. Tracy wasn't going to wear black or a dark color; her outfit would be bright and colorful - just like Missy's personality. This would remind her of the love she had for her dear friend.

Then, Tracy went on to explain how she had changed her thoughts after the death of her friend. She realized that we aren't promised to live forever and that life is very short. Tracy was going to think about food differently. Instead of filling her body with junk, she made the decision to treat her body better so that she might live a long life! She was going to be grateful for each day that she was alive.

I felt Missy's presence in the room with us. Tracy's love for her friend helped Missy in the Spirit world be able to share her energy. Tracy's goosebumps were all I needed to know that her friend appreciated everything about Tracy. Missy's legacy lived on in Tracy; forever changing the way Tracy viewed her life.

I, just like Tracy, have learned to live life differently now that I understand that this life is not guaranteed. Before we journey on together, let me preface the remainder of this book by saying that I am not a grief expert. If you need help from a professional, please get help. What I am going to share with you is what I learned about life and the possibility of an afterlife while I experienced grief. This book may not be the book for you to deal with deep pain. What this book does do is give the reader a different way to look at death and learn how to connect to a spiritual world - one that I discovered while searching for answers about death. It's a different way to live and I hope you enjoy the stories.

The magic of connecting with our loved ones seemed impossible to me at first. It's in my gratitude practice and belief in "something" that allowed me to live my life each day as though everything is a miracle. I sort of believed in signs before my parents died, but through my grief, I learned how deep this connection is. I also experienced the magic of connecting where my relationships (with my mother especially!) were healed and I let go of the pain and emotions of anything that didn't serve me.

Loss and grief show up in our life in many ways, not only death. It showed up in my life when my kids moved out, when I switched jobs or even when letting go of physical objects. My grief for my mother was very different from losing my father. With my mother, my grief was for never having a strong mother-daughter relationship. For my father, my grief was more about both of my parents gone. I was too busy making plans and taking care of their estate. These feelings of grief appeared years later and I didn't exactly know how to handle all of my feelings.

In this book, you are going to hear stories about people connecting with their loved ones in the spirit world- which I think is magical. Through my search for understanding grief and the signs of after-life, I am forever grateful to know these people and for them sharing their stories of deep connections to their loved ones. They are magical and most definitely show a connection to "something" more than we may ever fully comprehend. They guide us along this journey of life and most likely may spark changes in your life that you may not have expected. When we look beyond our physical world into this invisible layer of love, our hearts feel better and our lives are richer.

# 3

## The Power of a Name

Since the day I was born, it seemed my mother and I did not see eye to eye on a lot of things. I worried so much when I was about to share my book with the world; even though she wasn't technically here on earth in a physical body. I felt her around me but in a very different way. She had told me years ago not to write down anything "embarrassing" so I never dared to express my feelings on paper. My first book came from my soul and as I poured out my story onto the page, the fear of what I shared glowed within me like a small fire.

As humans, we at times seek our worthiness from outside ourselves. We look to our parents as young children and then we turn to our jobs, constantly looking for acceptance and validation that we are important. I was no exception. My mother never once said to me, "Congratulations! I'm so proud of you!" I stored this disappointment and memory inside my subconscious for many years.

I believe that when people arrive in what I call "the other side"- where the soul/consciousness lives without a body, they understand some of their mistakes. Each person does a life review to see what their soul learned during this lifetime. This information helped change my relationship with my Mom after she transitioned to spirit.

I wasn't sure if I would be able to connect with my Mom because I'm pretty sure she didn't believe in people who were gone communicating with the people left here on earth. Boy, was I ever wrong!

As a past life regression therapist, I have had clients that when guided to their in utero time and asked what they sense emotionally from their mother, they respond with things like, "She is anxious. I can see that she wasn't sure about having another child. That would make four children and she was nervous about having so many kids to take care of." or "She is excited to meet me but also nervous about being a mom for the first time." or "She is anxious and overwhelmed."

Since my mother had experienced such a traumatic experience with me in utero, my mother passed on some of her emotional trauma from that moment of deep grief- her anguish was floating within my blood.

What's scary about love is that we may get hurt. My mother loved her father so much that the pain she felt at his sudden death was very overwhelming. The pain of losing our loved ones changes our lives in ways we may never understand. I believe my mother changed the day her father died and then again on the day my father almost died of a heart attack- about 13 years after she lost her father to the same disease.

Subconsciously, when we are in pain, we reach for safety. Our hearts hurt and we search for a life without despair or grief. Brene Brown describes what my mother felt and the internal vibrational energy I had carried with me for so many years when she describes anguish- the "unbearable and traumatic swirl of shock..."

My mother didn't have the tools or resources to understand all of the emotions our hearts and bodies feel. The tools in my toolkit now have helped my body heal and be able to experience joy each and every day instead of keeping those same stories in my bones and cells.

I didn't understand why I couldn't be happy on Mother's Day. I loved being a mom and I loved watching my new daughter-in-laws become mothers. I got curious about my thoughts and discovered grief was hiding inside me. I didn't recognize it until I was ready to release my shield of protection.

As picture after picture appeared in my Facebook feed, I realized something. Someone posted, "I miss my Mom in Heaven." or "I love my Mom so much." Along with pictures of mothers and daughters together, getting pedicures or just being together, it finally hit me.

I was jealous and still in grief- a different type of grief. The grief I had was that I never had the kind of relationship with my mom that I wanted and I never would because she was gone. And, the even worse thought- if I was to be totally honest- which I never wanted to share my true self- was I did not miss my mom. This feeling was filled with shame and guilt. Did this mean that I didn't love my Mom? Was I a bad person because of this? Wasn't a child supposed to love their parents?

The shame that I felt was overwhelming. Brene Brown states that shame can't survive if we share it and bring it out into the open. When we do this, we are being our true selves and allowing others to see us. It's like it dissolves because it isn't hidden anymore.

Shame focuses on who I am as a person- "I am bad". I felt like I was a bad person because I didn't miss my mom. Guilt is the judgment I gave on myself. I was a bad person because maybe I failed in my relationship with my mother.

The key to shame and guilt is self-compassion. Could I forgive myself for having these feelings and thoughts? Could I let them go as they were no longer necessary or serving me? Was I worried what others would think of me if I shared these deep seeded feelings?

After I wrote my first book, my mother began to connect with me in ways we never did when she was here in physical form. Since the after-life is all about love, that is what I began to feel.

I was so excited to discuss the marketing side of my book release. My book had been born like a baby and, after writing for exactly nine months, it was ready to meet the world. I ordered copies through my publisher but I wanted a copy ASAP. I overnight shipped it on Amazon and waited patiently for the package to arrive. What a feeling of accomplishment! My hope was that my story would help someone somewhere understand that signs from Heaven are really possible.

The same day that I received a copy of my book, my new marketing agent called to learn more about me and my book. The marketing agent and I talked about my book and my wishes for distribution and marketing. At the very end of our hour-long conversation I felt bad because I had forgotten her name.

"I'm so sorry," I said. "I forgot your name." I knew she had said it quickly in her voice message the day before. "What is your name again?"

"Deanna," she replied. I gasped into the phone. My mother's name was Deanna. This simple coincidence for me meant that I received my mother's approval, the thing that had eluded me when she was living. My marketing agent spelled her name differently than my mom, but I did not know it at the time. Love and light surrounded me and I felt my mom said to me the words I had longed for when she was alive. "Congratulations! I'm so proud of you!"

DeeAnna was even "dimed" after she learned about my story.

"I have to tell you this story," she wrote in an email. When I phoned her, she was so excited.

"I went for a hike with my boyfriend. It was so weird. I found these two random dimes on the trail in the middle of the woods. I thought of you finding your dime on the mountain after your Dad passed. Anyways, I sort of forgot about it until my boyfriend proposed on top of the mountain! Finding the dimes on the trail made the day extra special. I felt like someone was there with me that day."

I was so happy for DeeAnna and felt such a deep connection with her. When looking for signs, always pay attention to names! They are a great way for Spirit to connect!

When you see your loved ones' name on a street sign, on the TV, or anywhere, know they are there with you. One time, I was watching TV and the name of the reporter was James Palmer. What are the chances? I knew my father was with me.

My friend Barb's husband transitioned to spirit after a long battle with multiple sclerosis. Barb cared for Ric during his last few years and missed him dearly after he left his physical body. Although she thought she felt his presence, she never seemed sure of any true signs from Ric.

About a year after Ric's death, she read my book and our friendship was rekindled.

I visited Barb a few years prior to writing my book. Since I hadn't seen Barb for years, I actually didn't know Ric was ill. After chatting in the kitchen, Barb directed me toward the sunroom to say hi to Ric. I wondered at the time why Ric couldn't just come into the kitchen to say hi, but I walked over to see him anyways. Ric was propped up in a wheelchair and could only move his head. Covering my initial shock, I put on my cheery face as I talked to Ric.

"Hey Ric. How are you?" I asked, which I immediately regretted. Anyone looking at him could tell that he wasn't well.

"Good, and you?" He responded with a more positive attitude than I imagined.

When I walked into the room, there was a different energy in the air. There was nothing to see but the feeling in the air was there. I wondered if Ric would transition soon.

I quickly wrapped up our short conversation and returned to the safety of the living room where the other women were gathering for our women's group. Ric passed away but not for several months after my visit.

About a year after Ric's death, Barb and I reconnected, and she welcomed me into her home to talk about the things she learned in my book, *Dimes from Heaven*. When I walked into her house, the energy in the air was palpable. Was she aware that Ric was right here with her? For a person who doesn't feel things the way I do, it's difficult to explain. It's like a vibrating energy within my body where I feel such happiness and love. I'm never quite sure how people will respond and I don't want to diminish their grief by saying something like, " Ric is right here!" I understand that not everyone feels as connected to this other dimension as I do. Some people envision it as a "haunted" house- one where the spirit of the deceased might do bad things. Reframing our vision of the after life takes time. One has to let go of the ideas presented to us in mainstream media. The other side is filled with unending love.

One day when I called Barb, she explained that today was difficult because it was Ric's birthday. She always missed him a bit more on this day. Don't we all miss our loved ones on special days? Christmas? Thanksgiving? Anniversaries? The empty chair sits there to remind us they are no longer here with us.

"Did he send you any signs?" I asked.

"Not that I know of," she laughed. " I didn't find any dimes." That's not the only way signs appear, I thought as I listened to Barb tell me all about her new car. She really wanted to make sure that I knew that she loved the color of it.

I knew he would give her a sign if she allowed herself to "see." When we look for signs, we have to open up our own energy to have faith and believe. We might not know how or when the sign will appear.

"I just love my new car because of the particular color red," she explained.

As the conversation moved on to talk about other things, I let go of the need to find a sign for Barb. It's not my job. Barb will either see it or not and I have no idea what the sign might be. She didn't ask for anything specific so it may be more difficult for her to recognize a sign.

A few days later, we were talking again and Barb said, "My son, Adam, looked up the name of the red color for my new car. You know, he has access to all of the specific colors for his car detailing business."

Why would Barb feel the need to have the exact name of the color? Why couldn't the color just simply be "red"?

"The color is grant maroon," Barb told me, not yet "seeing" the sign.

Barb's last name is Grant; which she took when she married her husband. Her three sons would always carry on the Grant name.

"That's it! That's your sign from Ric! You took the Grant name when you married Ric. The car color is a sign from him!" I explained to Barb, excited that she got a sign from her husband. Her seemingly innocent curiosity was spirit guiding her. She followed her intuition and her son just happened to be in the car business to have access to the exact color name for her new car and, of course, she was connected to me who would help her understand this was a sign, proving her continued connection with her husband.

"I never thought of it like that. Maybe you are right!" Barb sounded surprised. Barb's wish for a sign from her beloved husband was "Granted" through the power of a name, just like my mother "granting" her approval of my book.

# 4

## Have you been "Dimed"?

"It doesn't mean that we're sad the rest of our lives, it means that 'grief finds a place' in our lives. Imagine a world in which we honor that place in ourselves and others rather than hiding it, ignoring it or pretending it doesn't exist because of fear or shame."
~Brene Brown.

"Dimed" is a phrase I coined to explain when a person either receives a dime or a different sign from spirit. You can be "dimed" with a dime or "dimed" with a butterfly or "dimed" with a heart-shaped rock. A lot of times, after someone hears my story, their loved ones send them a dime because now Spirit knows they might believe in the invisible communication system. When we believe, our stories spread faith and can start a chain reaction with signs from Heaven.

It took me five years to be able to have the courage and strength to stop by the family camp on the lake that we sold after both of my parents passed away.

My grief was still raw. It was right there on the surface; ready to pop open like a water balloon being sliced open with a knife. I was longing for days gone by and felt like a lost child without my parents. The tears burst out as I remembered our times at camp. I always felt I let my Dad down by selling the camp. The camp was his pride and joy; handed down through three generations.

I hadn't planned to stop. I was doing my normal drive by when I threw my car into park and jumped out of the car. I love to drive the camp road; flashbacks of swimming and barbeques remind me how lucky I was to live on a small Vermont lake in the summer. It's time. I gather my courage and wonder if the new owners would remember me.

Dean is standing next to his truck and he immediately recognizes me after I introduce myself. He and his grandson are working on the dock today. As we walked down the hill toward camp, I was grateful for Nancy's warm welcome as she stepped out the back door.

Why did it take me so long to stop by? Why was I so worried? The answer- grief; a sense of loss and guilt for selling the property had consumed me. They had torn down the old camp to build something new. Change is hard and camp reminded me that my parents were no longer with me here on earth. My life changed so much the day they both left their physical bodies and returned to the spirit world.

My heart feels the pull of memories. Grief arriving like a tidal wave crashing over my whole body. It hits you when you least expect it and when you think you have it under control, something happens that either breaks your heart or fills your heart with incredible love. Walking on the land that I grew up on filled my heart with great sorrow but when I allowed love to flow freely, the tears seemed to sooth my aching heart.

I envisioned the camp the way it was when I last walked inside. I can hear the creaks in the floor and the porch door slam shut behind me. I can see the unfinished wall in the bathroom. There was no sheetrock; just two by fours standing as if waiting for the hammer and nails. I can see the "WOMEN" sign on the bathroom door that confused many people. If this bathroom is only for women, where do the men go to the bathroom? We would laugh as we said in unison, "Outside!"

Nancy and Dean shared how much they enjoy this spot on the lake. Nancy said that the camp was on "the right side of the lake." On the other side of the lake, the mountain blocked the sun in the afternoon and one couldn't see the beautiful sunsets that they see from this side of the lake. I smiled as my father would agree with them. Was my father there with us enjoying this conversation? I know I couldn't see his physical body but I seemed to sense something in the air.

When they tore the camp down, a lot of the wood was rotten. Yes, I think. We always suspected this but of course my father never wanted to look within. Sometimes when we look within, we find old, outdated things that are no longer needed; metaphorically speaking.

At some point there was a fire within the wall near the fireplace. I suspected such a thing but I honestly had no way of knowing this. They understood my surprise at this information and I felt any worries melt away. A smoldering fire inside the wall that by some miracle had not burned down my father's pride and joy. I secretly send a thank you to the Divine for stopping what could have been a very painful loss for my father.

Nancy wanted to show me the beautiful new house they built. I hesitated; unsure if I was ready to take this next step. It is actually a physical movement walking but it feels like I have to let go of the past as I walk into this new reality. The new world is built on the foundation that my father built. Family values are always within me and, even without our old family camp, I feel my roots steady and secure. As I walk and talk, I feel a new life opening up; one where I am able to explore a new way to live.

I imagined the old brown picnic table where our family crowded around with paper plates piled high with hotdogs and potato salad. Each year we would sing happy birthday to my boys as I tried to light the candles with the breeze from the lake blowing them out one by one. July birthday celebrations always included a party at camp with boat rides and swimming with their friends in the lake. I let go of the past to walk into the present, opening up a new chapter in my life. One where I transformed my heartache to feel love.

Before we walked toward the camp, I shared with Dean and Nancy about my books. I handed them a copy of both books and they felt honored to accept them. I turned to the page in the book and showed the oldest picture of camp from the 1940's when my Great Grandmother purchased the camp. They loved the books and looked forward to reading my story about the dimes.

As we stepped into the new front door and took a few steps in, I imagined my parents' bedroom to the left; where their new bedroom is now located. I can see the new blue rug my parents put in the room in the 1980's but my mind is in two worlds. One is the new room where new people live, but my mind travels to a distant memory; a part of me that never forgets. The antique claw bathtub is long gone and new flooring and sheetrocked walls create a beautiful new space.

Grief likes to do this. It's difficult to be in the moment because my mind wants to go back to the past, where my heart reminds me of the good times we had together.

The 1970's yellow refrigerator and stove would have been about where my feet were. The marshmallows were always in the white metal cabinet above the stove. Nancy directed me to the large bathroom but my brain remembers the red countertop and big sink where we used to spend time washing and drying dishes by hand. There was no dishwasher at camp. As I remember this, I realized that was part of the magic of camp. It slowed us down in our busy lives. It taught us to be together and to be present in the moment. Memories continued to pull at my heart strings creating a sense of nostalgia for times gone by.

My grief changed as we toured the newly built camp. My heart feels full and my eyes do not leak the tears that I thought might appear. Nancy's excitement makes me feel such positivity that I don't seem to have the sadness I thought I might. I sense love all around me. Gratitude surrounds me as the sun glistens through the many windows where the lake and mountain appear in perfect view. The gratitude is for both the past and the present. The memories of the past are always within me and now I can enjoy being with the new owners in this time and place. It's truly magnificent to see and I am overwhelmed by the beauty. The outside world transforms my insides from dark to light. I have to imagine a better feeling within myself. In Heaven there is no anger. This tour helps me release my guilt and feel my father's forgiveness within me.

We walk upstairs and as we do, I imagine Nancy's grandchildren enjoying sleepovers at the lake. There is a loft with many beds. It brings back memories of spending the night at camp with friends or with my own children. The loft is peaceful and inviting with the new bedding and slanted ceiling. At camp we imagine that the world is far away and it gives us time to spend with each other. My roots continue to feel strong as these memories are always a part of me.

I know enough about the afterlife now that my father is with me during the tour. He is not angry with me at all. He never was. The anger I felt was on a human level and I worried way too much! It was time to let this worry go. I believe that as soon as our soul transforms back to a spiritual essence, there are no judgements or regrets and all of our problems when we were here on earth are gone. All is well and our loved ones want us to know and feel the love from within.

As I descended the stairs to the basement, I realized that even though the ceiling racks where the kayaks hung and the old red white and blue striped waterskis from my youth are gone, they are always a part of me. Good memories solidified in my mind like a good movie. They are replaced with Nancy and Dean's new couches, pine walls and a wood stove to keep the room toasty warm.

Another bedroom to the back of the house and a full bathroom with laundry. Can you imagine? A washer and dryer at camp! I imagine my Mom carrying the dirty laundry in the cream colored plastic laundry basket back home to wash and then the clean clothes neatly stacked when we returned to camp.

I was completely filled with love as Nancy and I continued chatting in the kitchen. She was thankful for the books; I was thankful for the love and care for the land and camp they purchased from our family. I envisioned her family enjoying their time here; happy that they are making memories for generations to come.

Nancy invited me to stop by anytime - even if I want to sit on the lawn and just look at the mountain. She understood that I was still missing my Mom and Dad. Maybe more than I wanted to admit.

Fear inside me bubbles up at her offer. If I do sit on the lawn and look at the mountain, I might open up that grief bubble I have so carefully buried within me. What if I open it up? Will it ever stop? Will the tears overflow and I may be unable to stop the rush of water? I built a beautiful damn for my grief that keeps it safe and secure inside of me.

I've been trained to bury my grief. At times, I even put up a wall to protect myself from more pain. When I used to do this, I was not able to connect with the Spirit world. Acceptance lingers as I adjust to a new life without my parents. It's pulling me in a new direction. What if I believed that life is everlasting and my parents are always with me? What if I choose to cry but then feel amazing because they have sent me so many signs?

I thought of the dimes as I walked away from my tour. I felt an unseen force of energy as if my parents along with my Grandparents and Great Grandmother were there with me during this visit to the land I remember as a child. My grief shifted from sadness to love during that visit.

There seems to be something magical that happens after someone hears my dime stories. After my visit to camp, it sets in motion a series of coincidences for Nancy and Dean.

Nancy sent me a private message a few days after my visit. "You'll never believe what happened after your visit!"

Nancy and her daughter were "dimed". When they went to get their cart at the grocery store, a dime was stuck in the top part of the cart! How does a coin get stuck in the top of a metal grocery cart? Wouldn't it fall down in between the bars? How was it in the particular cart that Nancy and her daughter chose? Right after they learned about my dime story?

It's one thing to find a dime on the ground or near some other coins. This coin seemed to be carefully placed for them to find. I envisioned my father saying, "I'm glad you went to see the new owners. Make sure to forgive yourself. It's important to move on."

I always enjoy hearing stories when people are "dimed". Positive energy is contagious and when I shared my story with others, the energy spread like the wind blowing all around the world. I learned to connect to a totally different energy than ever before. One that is filled with love and does not focus on regrets. Every lesson in life is perfect and as the universe unfolds its plans, I allow myself to see beyond this physical world and look at life as a more mystical, spiritual journey.

Months later, Nancy would be "dimed" again. I wouldn't hear the story directly through Nancy though. The story would come through a mutual friend; someone who knows that souls who have crossed over show us signs every single day.

My friend, Ellen, sent me the following message, "So, I have this client that I've been doing his hair for years...he was telling me about his father-in-law passing away last week...we chit chatted about signs,etc and we both were like ya, we totally believe in that... 'the family that we bought the camp from...Monica...' I stopped him and said, 'Oh my God, Monica Morrissey??!!' I have been hearing about the renovations they have been doing in this camp they bought on Elmore since day one and I never knew it was your family's!!!!! So how we got started on this was that at the grave site...he saw something silver and shiny but didn't get a chance to look...he and his wife were talking about it later so they decided to go back....and sure as heck...it was a dime!! I love how the universe works!! And, he was going to tell me that you wrote a book about dimes from heaven. ..but I already knew!!!"

Ellen's story validated even more what Ellen and I already knew. Ellen and I had attended many of Rebecca Locicero's events called Messages from Heaven™. Rebecca Anne LeCicero is a talented and well-known medium featured in the Netflix movie series *Surviving Death*. She volunteers for the Forever Family Foundation. (https://www.foreverfamilyfoundation.org/) and has her own local TV show in Connecticut. During the evening event, Rebecca delivered messages from loved ones who have crossed into the Spirit world to help those of us left behind. Often it is exactly the message the loved one needed to hear to move forward with their life on earth. Rebecca uses all of her senses to help her understand the messages from Spirit. She asks for the audience to respond with only a yes or no as she does not want any extra information from the audience which might create doubt. Rebecca offers names, dates, numbers, significant objects, and even messages about the way the person died.

Ellen lost her dear sweet niece at the age of twenty-seven and her father at the age of seventy-two. (interesting as I write this, I noticed the numbers are reversed - a message right now from both of them?) One time, Ellen's father came through at an event. Rebecca kept looking between Ellen and myself. She was confused. Spirit kept telling her we were family but we said we actually were not related. We weren't family but our families were so connected that Ellen's father wanted us to know that he cared about all of our families. Ellen's niece, Samantha, was our next door neighbor.

Many people send me dime stories. The random dime makes them think of me. I try to explain that the dime isn't necessarily from my father. It is a way for their loved one to get their attention. It's like the first key they get and the door to Heaven cracks open. In time, the door can be unlocked with their own signs. Nancy's father was reaching out to her to say, "Hey, here is a dime to help you believe that I am still here." Then, he may use other signs after that to show that he is able to communicate with her. Nancy can try to figure out what her key is. It may be something other than a dime. It should be something that is meaningful to her and her father. This has the power to transform the pain of her loss to love and connection.

I worried so much that my father would be angry with me because I sold the camp but this meant that I missed out on enjoying peace throughout my day. Here are some suggested things to do to bring your loved ones closer to you.

- Do you have regrets with a loved one? Write about it and let it go. You are forgiven. Your loved one wants you to know this. The energy of your writing will bring your loved ones closer to you.
- Visit a place that reminds you of your loved one. Remember the love and the good memories like my friend Tracy. Think of a favorite memory.

Recently, my Uncle was dimed. It was the day before it would have been his dear wife's eightieth birthday. We lost Aunt Jean to cancer nine months before. When my Uncle found the dime, he said, " Jimmy sent me a dime." It may have been from my dad but it may have been sent from his wife! She knew that my Uncle would recognize that the dime was a key to Heaven!

The keys to Heaven are available to everyone. Your energy, your beliefs, and your thoughts are the keys to opening the invisible door to another dimension.

# 5

## Numbers and Intuition

**"Love and life remain within us, and the potential for meaning is always there."** ~David Kesslar

Threes had never been my number, but threes were about to teach me a lesson about my intuition and the clairaudience whisper I hear from Spirit.

It was the summer of 2020 and repeating threes kept showing up for me. I would wake up in the night and the clock read 3:33 or I would check the time during the day and it would be 3:33. Threes would appear on license plates or on addresses. Threes seemed to be appearing out of nowhere, surprising me like a shooting star. I asked the universe, "What is the message?" I didn't hear or feel any message, so I sort of forgot about it.

My husband, my son, my son's wife (who was his girlfriend at the time) and I rented a camp on a lake for a week. I love the water and remember all the years I lived on the lake in the summertime. I felt like I needed a break and some time away. I absolutely love to swim and be out on our boat. Summers are short where I live in Vermont and I wanted to enjoy the sunshine and fresh air. It would be fun to be together on the lake. My son moved out of our house about three years prior and we all were looking forward to spending time together.

Soon after we arrived at the camp, my son's dog introduced us to the neighbors. Dogs aren't afraid of going over to say hi to strangers. My son began chatting with one of the neighbors. My heart was filled with pure joy as I watched my twenty-four year old engage in a conversation with a stranger.

I overheard parts of their conversation. Joel, the neighbor, shared about how they remodeled the camp when they bought it a few years ago. Since my son is a lineman, he was interested in hearing about the electricity and Joel shared all about the updates. They discuss things that I don't know anything about.

There is peace as I watch my son interact with Joel. Patrick is respectful, kind, and caring. There is something about the far away look in Joel too but I can't quite put my finger on the feeling I seem to be picking up on. He seemed so kind to my son but also had this distant look in his eyes.

As we talked, we discovered we have a mutual friend. His wife is a hairdresser and she is friends with my friend, Ellen. (yes! The same Ellen from earlier!) I heard this little voice inside my head, "Tell them about your books." My analytical part of my brain responded to the whisper, "Just because these people knew Ellen, and Ellen likes my books, doesn't mean they are interested in my dime story! Why would I tell complete strangers about my books?" I kept wondering if this idea came from their connection with Ellen or if there was another reason.

The week goes on and we chatted here and there with Tammy and Joel. The dog enjoys playing fetch on their lawn. They fed him a few treats when walking down to the water. We enjoyed our week on the lake and our time away from work.

Learning how to tune in to my intuition and turn away from my ego is a big lesson for me. Intuition comes from a feeling and a different voice within. For me, it's repeated whispers like when I was given the message to go find the lost penny in the armchair on the day of my father-in-law's passing. Intuition gently guides me in my life. Ego comes from a place to make me feel important or better than another person. I use the following messages to figure out if the message is from my intuition or my ego.

Is the message positive? Spiritual guidance is never negative or punishing.

Is the message given in a spirit of love and kindness? Does the message guide myself or others to live differently? With more peace and gratitude?

I thought my intuitive guidance to share my book was coming from a sense of bragging, which is my ego wanting notoriety for being an author. What if they thought I was being pushy about my book? All week long the whisper would not stop.

Joel finished his yoga routine on the grass near the edge of the lake. As I packed a cooler into the car, Joel stopped to chat on his walk back to his house.

"I wanted to live on the water. That's why we bought this place. We turned a very old camp into our new home," he shared and I thought about my old family camp being turned into a new home.

"I grew up on the water in the summer. I wanted to come stay on the lake so that I could relax during all this COVID craziness. I needed to shut off technology and just get centered," I explained. Then I said something that still sounds weird when I say it. I said, "I am a writer and I needed a reset to shut off from work. I wanted to sit by the water and decide what to write about next."

"What do you write about?" Joel asked me and I felt a sense of relief that he is interested. This released that voice as the pressure had been building all week long. My head seriously felt like Old Faithful about to erupt. For some reason, I felt the need to share this information with Joel and I had no idea why.

"Well, I wrote two books. The first one is called *Dimes From Heaven*. It's a cool story about some dimes that my father sent to me after he died. One dime I even found on top of a mountain! I can't tell you where the other dime was found because I don't want to ruin the ending of the book," I focused on the dime story, not about being an empath.

"Oh wow. That's pretty cool," Joel responded as his eyes looked beyond me toward the calm, smooth lake.

I'm never quite sure how people will react to my story. Will Joel be interested in my story? Mostly I connect with women. Do men believe in signs from Heaven too?

Joel then surprised me when he shared that he receives signs but his signs aren't dimes. "I lost my son a few years ago. He was twenty-one years old when he was in an accident. My son showed me the number 333. He died at 3:33 in the morning. I read it on his death certificate. The address to this property is 333."

I can't believe it. I ignored the whisper telling me to share my book all week long. Now, I understood why I was being guided to tell Joel about my dime story.

"Oh my gosh. I have been seeing threes all week! I had no idea why. Well, that explains it!" I am astonished but sad as he shared about his son's death. The pain of losing a child crushes my heart. Joel's grief floats through the air.

"Would you like a copy of my book?" I spontaneously offered him a free copy.

"Yes, I would love a copy of your book. I truly believe in the signs," Joel said.

Joel believed that Jared was with him always and forever. I wrote "Believe" in the book I gave to Joel, but Joel truly believed it already. I hope he enjoyed my story. His son is with him always and forever.

I shared with my son the story of Joel's son. We do the math. Joel's son would be the same age as my son. Was that what I was seeing when Joel and my son were talking? Was Joel wondering what his son would have been like had he still been alive?

It took me almost a week to listen to that little voice inside me telling me to share about my books. When I did, I figured out why I had been seeing 3's for weeks. His son knew I was coming to that camp and he knew that his father believed. I believe it was Joel's son whispering in my ear, "Tell my dad about your books."

When events, numbers or signs repeat over and over again, it is a way for spirit to get our attention. Divine guidance can be about anything, not just numbers or messages from Spirit. If you are having health issues and you happen upon three different articles about cutting out caffeine, that might be the answer you were searching for. One time, I had three different people tell me about a book they just read. I took that as a sign that I was supposed to read that book! I wasn't sure why but it didn't matter. Spirit was sending me a message and I needed to be willing to listen.

I'm glad Joel knows that his son is with him all the time. I enjoy listening to these stories but also feel the heartbreak when we lose our loved ones. It's comforting to be able to feel the love in the midst of missing his physical body.

On the day we were packing to leave, Joel and his wife were driving by the camp. They stopped to say hi and then Joel said with a big grin on his face, "Monica, I thought of you this afternoon. I looked at the clock and it was 3:33."

Joel and I had connected in such a powerful way. I still think of him often but especially whenever I see repeating threes.

This experience helped me to learn how to distinguish between my critical, problem-solving mind and my intuition. There are a few ways to tell the difference.

Our intuitive guidance comes from both our minds and our bodies. Close your eyes and take a few deep breaths. As you relax your body, begin to relax your mind. When your mind is quiet, think of some time where "you just knew something". When you have that feeling, where in your body do you feel it? In your gut? In your heart? throat? A lot of people feel it in their gut but I feel it in my heart. Then figure out where the voice is coming from. Usually, there is a pattern to this voice. It may be coming from the right, left, or center of your mind. Start to tune into this like you are receiving a signal from a radio. If the guidance comes from a place of love, listen. It is guiding you in your life.

I learned how to be in touch with this positive spiritual part of myself through my connection with my father. We are all here to learn our soul lessons. Sometimes the lessons seem so difficult that we don't know how to keep on living. When a loved one is taken away from us, life seems unbearable. It was through the pain of losing someone I loved dearly that I was able to learn to live my life differently.

When I first met Joel, I had no idea the pain he lives with each and every day. I'm sure he misses his son. I believe we choose our parents when our soul enters earth school. Lessons are learned for everyone when we lose a young person. It reminds us that tomorrow is never promised so we need to enjoy each moment for what it is: "a present". Each day is a gift. I think of this when I go places. I sometimes let people go in front of me in line at the grocery store. You would be surprised at how this little gesture means so much to people. Another thing that I love to do is give compliments to people. This simple thing changes a person's day and makes my day better.

Since meeting Joel, I have had three - three penny days! And they all have to do with following my intuition while parking my car. A simple daily task that helps me feel connected to Heaven.

I used to choose my parking spot in a very different way than I do now.

I used to try to find the closest parking spot to wherever I was going. Then, my insurance agent explained that most accidents happen when backing up, especially from a parking spot. He suggested always parking in a spot where I would be able to drive out without backing up and to park further away from other cars. Then, I became thoughtful about more movement throughout my day so I decided to park further from the destination to be able to take a short walk. Now, I think of these things, but sometimes at the last minute I decide to switch my choice of where to park. This little change in the way I live has had such a profound effect on my life; showing me how to let my intuition guide me each and every day.

On this particular day, I picked a spot further away from the other cars. As I was getting out of the car, I noticed two people who attended one of my book events. I had known them for years and the gentlemen even won a dime necklace at my book launch party! I thought it was fitting that a minister won the dime necklace - truly a message from my Father as to how important Faith was to him. I said hi and then I looked down. My friends were about 20 feet away and this was during the beginning of COVID so we were keeping our distance. I told them I just found 3 pennies! I think there must be one for each of us! I picked them up and began to look at the years. They choose their pennies based on the meaning of the year. The two they picked were very significant to them - I can't remember if they were birth years or their anniversary. We were all so happy! We believed that these pennies were truly, "Pennies from Heaven!"

Later that fall, my sister, Merrilee and I went to visit my Aunt and Uncle, my Mother's brother. For me, pennies are always a sign from my Mom. We met at a local grocery store and I drove everyone to see my Aunt and Uncle. I parked on the right side of my sister Debbie's car and she hopped in the back seat. We had a great visit and then we headed back to drop Debbie off at her car. Instead of parking on the right side of the car, like I did earlier, at the last minute, I decided to park on the left side. I put the car in park and my sister proceeded to step out of the car. Debbie went to put her foot down and said, "Merillee, look at what is near my foot!" It was a penny! That was a sign from my Mom!

Instantly I thought, "well, she got a penny. Maybe I can find one too!" I jumped out of my car so fast that I didn't have time to rationalize my thoughts. Why would I think I would get a penny just because she found one? In less than two seconds, I listened to my intuition and didn't analyze anything.

I proceeded to open my door and guess what? There was a penny on my side of the car too! Mom gave us BOTH a penny! Then, in less than a millisecond, I decided that Merrilee needs a penny too....I opened my door again and looked really closely at the pavement. My penny was brand new so I saw it easily when the sun was shining on it. I looked harder this time. Sure enough, I found ANOTHER PENNY! I gave it to Merrilee and she said, "I never met your Mom!" I explained that it didn't matter. My Mom knew she was here with us now and she was sending love to all of us!

My Mom wanted all of us to know that she was sending support to her brother that day. I felt it, my Sister felt it and Merrilee felt it. We knew she was close to us.

I went home feeling good but also worrying about my Aunt, who was very ill. I prayed for her and her family. That night I had a dream. In the dream, I called my Grandmother, my Mother and Uncle's mother. I don't remember talking to her much about anything. I told my Grandmother I just called to say "Hi" Grandma. Dreams are a way for our loved ones to visit. When I woke up, I wondered what the message was. Instantly, I thought, my Grandmother wanted to let us all know that she, like my Mom, was with us to support us during this time and would take care of Aunt Jean when she transitioned to Spirit.

A few days later, Merrilee was worried about going on a trip. Her car was making a funny noise and she was worried something might happen. She called to tell me that she found a penny, thought of my Mom and she felt it was going to be ok to go on her trip. Her worry and anxiety melted away. They went on the trip and everything was fine, just like Merrilee's intuition had told her.

While working on this book, I had my third three penny day. I found my first penny at the chiropractor's office, where both of the chiropractors had graduated from 'Palmer' College. Palmer is my maiden name so I knew this was a sure sign from both of my parents! Then when I stopped for gas at a local store, I found a penny next to my car. As I walked toward the store, I saw what I thought might be another coin. It was so dirty that I thought it might be a dime or just a piece of trash. I almost didn't pick it up but decided it would be number three for the day. I picked it up and sure enough, it was another penny! I felt my Mom was supporting me while writing this book!

As I finished writing this chapter, I was filling out a form to send in the mail. The address was 333. Then, I opened up a piece of mail. There was a bill for $333.35. I will forever think of Joel and Jared whenever I see threes. And, I have learned how to listen to the guiding intuitive whispers from my soul.

# 6

## Heart Shaped Rocks and Four Leaf Clovers

One time I cut open a hard boiled egg and the shape of the yolk was a heart! Hearts had never really been my sign. I wouldn't always understand the meaning of different signs that began appearing in my life, until I learned to listen to my intuition and follow its guidance system like a GPS directing me to my destination.

I went for a hike up Elmore Mountain with a woman who went to my high school but we hadn't seen each other in years. She loved my book and wanted to connect about the topics I wrote about.

It was a beautiful day in Vermont. The greenery filled every part of the forest and the sixty degree weather was perfect for a hike. We chatted along the way and I enjoyed the time spent talking about what it is like to be an empath. We feel so deeply that at times it can be a challenge. The most important thing about being an empath is sharing our love; which we both do as we hike. As I hiked, an unusual thing happened on this particular day. It seemed that everywhere I looked, there was a rock shaped like a heart. I took a few pictures but then stopped. Hearts were sprinkled on that mountain like confetti sent from God.

I didn't think much about it until following my intuition guided me to a coincidence that was difficult to ignore, sending me a direct key to heaven's messages.

My husband's cousin had shared a dime story with me a week before my hike. It went something like this:

"I got your book a few weeks ago. Something interesting happened on the first day I got your book! I brought it in my car to the hospital where my husband was about to have surgery. I grabbed the book, stepped out of the car and, I kid you not, there was a dime on the ground. I thought that was kind of cool. Then I was about to get on the elevator, but it was so full, I decided to take the stairs. I couldn't believe it when I saw another dime- on the stairs! Then, after my husband's surgery, I was getting back into my car and~ you guessed it! Another DIME! It was a **THREE DIME DAY!** I actually didn't get to read much of your book that day, but I thought how coincidental it was that I find these dimes today! I had a feeling my husband was going to be okay for his surgery."

My intuitive whisper kept sending me a message over and over again. "Tell Molly that it is going to be okay." Until I send the message, the whisper seriously won't shut up. It keeps replaying like a stuck record- over and over, again and again. Finally, I sent her this message:

"Good Morning! So, when you were sharing your dime story, your Father kept popping up in my mind. All I kept hearing from him was, "It's going to be okay" every time you talked about being in the hospital and another dime. I have no idea how this all works, but I felt the need to share this with you! Luv ya! And hope everything goes okay today!" Now the voice inside my head was able to stop replaying the message.

On the day of my hike, Molly responded.

"Thanks Monica. There is so much of your book that rings true for me. My father usually sends me heart shaped rocks. We never talked about them as far as I can remember but I just know they are from him. He was always picking up interesting rocks and handing them to me. He also visited me in a dream once. After his death I was a mess. And I was a mess for years! I could not talk about him without crying and I was just so sad. So finally he came to me and said, 'Hey! I'm okay. I'm happy and you have got to get a hold of yourself and be happy too!' I woke up from that dream so relieved and so much more at peace."

Did she just write about heart shaped rocks?

"Oh my goodness! I went on a hike today and I saw so many heart shaped rocks! That is so cool. Now I know it was Uncle Doug. Check out these pictures. I did not know who was trying to get my attention!" I replied, excited that we discovered this connection.

She responds, "Oh my goodness. Yes. And don't even get me started on four-leaf clovers. I practically trip over them!"

A few days later, I hiked Elmore again. I saw a lot of heart shaped rocks. I knew that Uncle Doug was welcoming my dear Father-in-law to Heaven.

Molly's dream was very clear. Her dad was sending a message to her. When we sleep, we are able to let go of our rational mind and allow our subconscious, along with spirit, to send us messages. His message was clear. Our loved ones in Heaven want us to live our lives and be happy. They want the best for us. They don't want to see us be in so much pain. The more we turn toward love, the more they are able to connect with us.

I shared this heart-shaped rock story on my blog and the love would return to me with two boomerang events. I believe that when a person sends positive energy into the world, it comes back to them like a boomerang. The old saying, "You get what you give." is true with all things. Positivity was about to come right back at me.

Lynn was a teacher at one of the schools I worked at. She and I both had been in education for over thirty years and we knew that taking care of everyone's social and mental health was, at times, more important than math or reading. It is just as important to learn how to connect with nature, eat in a healthy way and take care of ourselves. We brought this passion to our work each and every day.

Lynn read my books and connected to many topics. In the summer, Lynn lives on an island on Lake Champlain, the biggest lake in Vermont. Lynn enjoyed taking care of the animals in the barn and caretaking for the rental property. The wind can howl during a storm but the calm of the lake at night is enough to quiet even the most active mind. The paths Lynn walked on the island connect her small log cabin to the beach shore, the barn and the rental house.

As Lynn walked the rocky trail from the log cabin through the woods to the barn, her mind was on other things. She had her phone with her and decided to check Facebook. That's exactly when it happened. As she opened up my blog post about heart-shaped rocks, she looked down and saw right in front of her a rock carefully placed on her path. There were many rocks on the path but one seemed to stand out in the pile. The rock wasn't the shape of a heart, but a heart seemed to be carved into the rock. A magical transformation made many years ago when the water swirled over and over through the rock to form the heart, showing the true beauty and power of nature.

I received this rock in the mail from Lynn and I knew the power of connection. I understood that the more I shared these amazing stories, the more love was in the world. Love was beginning to return to me like a boomerang more and more.

Another teacher I knew would then connect with me. Carrie and I taught at the same small elementary school in northern Vermont for twenty-four years. She retired during the pandemic, and, unfortunately, we were not able to have a retirement party for her. She always said that she wanted to write a book, so I thought *More Dimes From Heaven, A Journey to Self-Publishing* would be the perfect retirement gift for her. I hope she writes the book she always dreamed of writing.

We sat on her front porch and talked about life, work, school and memories of our own children growing up together. We talked about how life is such a gift and how important it is to enjoy every moment. It was so nice to sit and have time to talk with a friend, who was truly a role model for me throughout my years teaching.

"Life is so precious. You just never know what might happen tomorrow," I say and remember her dear sweet niece, Sam. Ellen and Carrie are sisters and they both felt such a big loss when Samantha transitioned to Spirit so young. I know how they feel because we lost Tyler so young.

As I was leaving and walking back to my car, I looked down and spotted a four-leaf clover. I debated about picking it and then decided I probably should. This is a critical moment when following my intuition. My first thought was to pick it but then my brain tried to convince me to do something different. When we let our intuition guide us, it is usually our first thought that is the better thought.

We are all connected in this world in ways that are surprisingly shocking and at times seem so incredible one may struggle to try to explain it using our linear thinking brains. We try to rationalize the unexplainable events that occur that just don't seem to make any sense to us. When Spirit is involved, there is no explanation other than we are connected with an invisible energy field, just like cell phones. There is no cord connecting us but we are connected to this mysterious and invisible communication system. Molly had set in motion some more signs from Spirit when she shared the words, "And don't even get me started on four-leaf clovers. I practically trip over them!"

As I gave it to Carrie, I wondered if the four-leaf clover was a sign for something. I suggested she put it in the book I gave her and walked away. I think it might be good luck for her book.

I hopped in my car and was ready to leave. My cell phone sat in my car while we chatted so that I wouldn't be distracted while we visited. I took a quick peek to see if I had any messages before I drove away. The message I received got me so excited that I ran back out to show Carrie.

"Carrie, you are never going to believe this message I just got!" She might have thought I won a million dollar lottery. It wasn't the lottery, but that's how excited I get when someone makes a connection to Heaven.

When I shared the message, she and I both knew that this was a sign from Heaven.

"Hi there- so I'm feeling like I need to write about my dad. I keep finding 4 leaf clovers... I know probs sound crazy... is this a real thing? I found the first one on the day he passed- a few hours before... but I keep finding them. Monica- life is so crazy right now... my world is turned upside down. I'm trying to stay positive but it's so hard..." ~Heather

This was within minutes of me finding the four-leaf clover that I gave to Carrie. We both smiled and I went on my way. We both felt Heather's pain deeply as Carrie and I have both lost our fathers. Within that pain and heartache, we knew that Heather felt her father was with her. It was beautiful that Heather now understands love from Heaven can be a simple coincidence.

Heather's family grew up on the lake right next door to our camp. She and I swam and played together during the summer months. I'm sure Lake Elmore is a part of her like it is me.

I explained to Heather that if she thinks it is a sign, then it is. We don't need verification or validation from anyone. It's our choice to believe in the signs.

Heather has since found 14 four-leaf clovers, 2 five-leaf clovers and 4 feathers. I know her heart is hurting because her dear father is no longer a physical part of her family. Her father is reaching out to her in such a different way. I know she can feel him in her heart. He is always with her.

This is how positivity spreads. One person at a time. One penny or dime at a time. When I shared the four leaf clover story to my sister she shared with me that some of her co-workers found four leaf clovers the very same day that I found the one at Carrie's house. These four leaf clovers were so big that she took a picture of them next to a dime. The dime looked miniature next to them! Spirit was having fun by making it such a big event to find gigantic four leaf clovers so that my sister and I would connect at the same time Heather was messaging me about her four leaf clovers.

Dimes are always my sign but Spirit kept showing me more and more signs; my heart expanding and guided towards love. Heather and Molly reached out to me for help in believing in signs from Heaven. All of these helping me understand the Spirit world more and more.

# 7

## Does the Other Side Watch Everything we do?

Angie moved from France to begin a new life in Canada. She was starting life fresh after she lost her husband to suicide. Friends helped her when life seemed unbearable and her heart was shattered.

I met Angie after writing my first two books and about the time I began doing Intuitive Angel Card readings. Since it had been years since her husband had passed, Angie wanted a new relationship with a man. I met her during COVID so it was a challenge to meet people. She also knew that something was holding her back but she didn't know what or why. She was struggling to move on even though she knew she wanted to.

I asked Angie if she would like an Angel card reading and maybe we might tap into some messages from her deceased husband. She was receptive and we set a date to work with James Van Praagh's card deck, *Talking to Heaven.*

The first card brought deep tears. "It was not your fault." Angie might have thought that maybe she could have done more for him. The woulda, coulda shoulda's filled her mind. Unconsciously, she might have thought she could do more for him but ultimately, she knew that she had done all that she could have for him. Forgiveness is a powerful message and Angie felt it deep within her. It was time for her life to move on.

The next card, "There is no such thing as death" revealed another incredible message. My mind instantly thought of a story to help Angie with this idea.

"Well, let's think about this for a minute. I want to tell you a story. When I was first married, my husband and I bought my Grandmother's house. I felt her all the time and worried about what she would think or say. I mean, we were newly-wed, if you get what I'm saying," I hinted at what I didn't want my Grandmother to see.

Angie and I both laughed as our minds wondered if Heaven watched everything we did.

"You need to understand that Heaven feels but doesn't see. It's their essence that is here but not their physical body with eyes watching every-thing we do. Your husband wants you to find someone to be with and wants you to know he promises not to watch," I explained to her.

Rivers of tears ran down her cheeks as she hadn't been aware that this may have been blocking her ability to have a new relationship with a man. She shared her worries that she would hurt her husband if she was with another man.

"I never thought about it but you're right. I feel him and know he is here with me. I am better able to understand this now and let go of this worry. I am so grateful for this authentic conversation about things like this that most people don't want to talk about. Thank you, Monica," Angie was filled with gratitude as we spoke the unspoken feelings we have after someone dies.

The last card was "Tears cleanse the soul" and the picture was a heart made with water droplets. Angie's tears created space within her to allow love to flow again. She had released an invisible block by tapping into her worries and letting go even more.

Another client who I met with had lost her father and she struggled a lot since his death. She buried her grief deep within her. The card "It's not your fault" is powerful in many situations. This woman had been holding on to blame for years. When I read the card, she immediately started crying and said, "I thought it was my fault that my baby died." The woman had a miscarriage and, in her grief, had kept this deep feeling to herself for many years. By releasing this guilt, I could tell she was ready to let it go. We never know what types of emotions we hold onto until we hear everyone's stories. Heaven wants us to let these feelings go and be able to enjoy living.

Grief hides out in ways that are difficult to understand. Once we share our true feelings with someone, it's like the shame and guilt dissolve, releasing the block we need to let go in order to connect to our loved ones.

# 8

## Remembering the Love

As I got closer to publishing, I called Jay to help with the cover of my book.

"Hey Jay, It's Monica. I'm writing this book and I really need a picture of Elmore Mountain. I was hoping you might have one I could use for the cover," I explained.

"Well, you can look at my Facebook page. I have a lot posted," he responded.

"Well, I was thinking of a daytime picture, not a sunset picture. I've seen lots of sunsets. Do you have any daytime pictures?" I asked, hoping he would say yes.

"No. I do mostly sunsets," he surprised me with his answer. "I think you should call this other photographer that I know." He gave me the name but it was meaningless to me. I knew I wanted a photograph of Elmore Mountain from Jay. Jay had done my High School senior pictures, my wedding pictures and we stayed connected through the years.

"No Jay. I want a picture from you. Each part of my book means so much to me. The cover is a piece that I would love for you to be a part of," I pleaded.

"Okay, Well. Is your book Spiritual at all?" he asked. If we had been in person, he would have seen my jaw drop and my eyes open wide as I smiled.

"Oh my....Yes! You have no idea how spiritual!" I said.

ONCE UPON A DIME

"Then I have the perfect picture for you. I just need to find it," he explained.

Relief washed over me and my happiness traveled through the phone line.

"Great! I can't wait to see this picture."

What could the picture be? What would make the picture spiritual?

For weeks and weeks I waited patiently. As Jay looked through hard drive after hard drive, he knew what he was searching for. He was determined to find this one picture his mind remembered.

When Jay finally found the picture, I thought he had altered it. Was that cross in the sky really in the original photograph? He assured me that the photo had not been altered. I needed more help though. The picture was great but I didn't have the necessary computer skills to create a book cover. Jay sent me some ideas and I absolutely loved them! It was the perfect cover for the book I never ever expected to write.

When it came time for my second book, I sent Jay another message.

"Any ideas?" I asked without even explaining what my book was about. I sent him some title ideas and he responded, "Let me sleep on it. I'll let you know."

A few days later, he said, "What about dimes floating around in the solar system?"

I couldn't believe it. It was exactly what the theme of my book was-being guided by the universe to write my books. Jay had no idea how perfect this was.

Jay died while I was writing this book. It was one of those deaths that shocked our community to our core. It was a homicide-suicide. Jay first shot his wife and then himself. I heard about it while at work and couldn't shake this agitated feeling. Since I was working, I didn't take the time to process my feelings and buried them like I had done for years. I watched myself process this and as I tried to stuff the sadness down, it suddenly appeared as anger. How could he do that? What was he thinking?

**"Death by suicide is not a selfish act or even a choice. It's a sign
of a mind that needs help." ~David Kessler**

Suicide wasn't new to me. I remember wanting to run away
when my mother told me my high school friend, Donna, had died by
suicide. I was sixteen years old and had never had someone close to me
die. I didn't even know she was suicidal. I didn't want to hear that news.
I didn't want my friend to be gone forever. My mother's tight grip on
my arm brought me to the reality that Donna was so bothered by life
she felt she needed to leave.

All kinds of woulda, coulda, shoulda's came to me. If I woulda done
this, maybe Donna wouldn't have done it. I coulda helped her if I only
knew. I shoulda spent more time with Donna. These all came flooding
back to me as I processed Jay's death.

**"Such thoughts are a product of guilt, but they are also the
mind's way of trying to assert control in an uncontrollable situation
that has already happened." ~David Kessler**

I personally knew what it felt like to be so depressed that I wasn't
sure I wanted to live. Several times in my life, I experienced such depression that I thought about suicide. I'm grateful that I had people in
my life who helped me dig myself out of my depths of sadness and that
I had made a conscious decision that I wanted to live.

I shared my first book with a friend and she returned the gift by
gifting me the book *The Untethered Soul* by Michael Singer. This book
helped me understand how my brain worked. The negative voice inside
my head was loud and clear in my first book- I was so scared to share
my story and share my spiritual side with the world. I was a public
school teacher and the rules of this responsibility to my profession were
inferred- I didn't feel that I would be allowed to show my true self
because I wasn't allowed to teach anything that might be considered
religious or spiritual. When I began to understand how that voice inside
my head worked, I began to understand a key to living a more loving
and accepting life.

Our brains were built to look for patterns in order to keep us safe. Years and years ago, the only way to survive was to remember that the tiger was dangerous. Nowadays, it is important that we understand how the amygdala is constantly working to try to keep us safe but also be able to access the prefrontal cortex to calm the amygdala down.

Since we are human and there are dangers here on earth, we were pre-programmed like a computer to survive the elements. So much so that the negative things that happen are like velcro in our brains and all of the positive things are like a teflon pan- they slip right off! The problem with this internal programming is that it has become dysfunctional, leading people to be in such a rut that they might not understand why their mind thinks like that. It's like the wires in our brains have become tangled so much that the system needs a spiritual re-boot. We aren't in survival mode but our brains are still functioning like we are.

We are hardwired for fight, flight or freeze so that we are able to stay alive. If a bear or a tiger chased us, we would be able to take action in order to survive. Now, our stresses are so different. Modern society has created a space where we are safe inside shelters and the food system has grown so much that most are able to shop for the food they need. The stress is now in the form of a student not understanding a math problem or being able to read. Teachers can go into fight or flight when an angry parent calls them. The worker at any business struggles with the daily stress of emails, phone calls or working long hours. And, when someone isn't nice to us, we think we are being rejected by the tribe- which could signal to our bodies that we wouldn't survive the situation. Our bodies know how important being a part of the tribe is for survival.

Our minds begin to create stories to help us combat the stress, creating a theory-evidence loop. The story is based on the evidence we have seen and then those stories begin to guide us in our life.

Our brains were built to look for patterns in order to keep us safe and they love to create stories- a full circle loop, beginning, middle and end. Years and years ago, the only way to survive was to remember that the tiger was dangerous. It is important that we understand how the amygdala is functioning in a different way in modern society- so much so that people are getting caught up in the stories their brains create.

I get caught up in what I call a "negative evidence loop". My brain was trained at a young age to see people as threats so I began searching for the evidence that would prove my theory correct. Of course, none of this was done consciously. It's the subconscious family programming that I grew up in. In order to retrain my brain, I had to do a lot of conscious work.

This is how my mind was programmed. Since my mother didn't trust people and spoke poorly about her friends, that's what I learned. I know it wasn't her fault and that is how generational trauma is passed down. The more I looked for problems, the more problems I created in my mind- creating stories to prove my theories. My mind didn't know how to search for the good things because I wasn't programmed for this.

Looking for good things takes practice- just like a soccer player practices their shot on goal. The first kick might be a fail but with practice, the shots get better and better.

My gratitude practice started out small. I remember the first night that I wrote my first gratitude. I seriously hadn't even remembered what I had done that day. The positive thoughts did not come easy. I had to search and search for them. How would I ever get positive thoughts to stick like velcro and the negative thoughts to slide away?

Practice. I had to practice looking for the good. I had to practice saying positive things when I was around other people. My practice shifted my evidence loop and grew more and more each day. Suddenly, I was thankful for the blue sky or the birds chirping. By writing ten things I was grateful for and ending my day with the one best part of my day, this helped velcro the good parts of my life into my subconscious.

I tried to grow broccoli one time in my garden. It grew but the harvesting totally creeped me out. I'm not a fan of worms or snakes and when you harvest broccoli, there are these big, green worms that are hiding out in the plants- similar to our thoughts hiding in our brains. These are the thoughts that we don't tell anyone.

I heard from a friend how important it was to put fresh broccoli into salt water. The reason to do this is to remove the hidden worms from the plants as they don't like the salt. As I looked over my plants, I wondered if my friend meant that *sometimes* there are worms. It seemed as though I didn't have any on my broccoli.

To be on the safe side, I decided to fill the bowl with salt water and see if any worms might wiggle away from the broccoli. I watched and nothing happened. I walked away and almost fifteen minutes later, there were several worms floating in the water. The worms had to be summoned off the broccoli. They were hidden and tricked me into thinking they weren't there.

This is how trauma is stored in our subconscious and how our negative thoughts need to be brought to the surface. We do this by allowing them to move out into the open with "salt". We face them by listening to them, maybe even sharing them with someone safe and then moving beyond the negative voice.

Emotions are only supposed to last for ninety seconds. Think about that. Think of a negative emotion that you are holding onto right now. What's that emotion about? Most likely it is about something that happened days, months or even years ago or it is worrying about something in the future. Ditch it. Throw it away. Stop engaging with it. Then, look around you and bring your body and mind into the present moment. If it is something big, get help releasing it.

Our bodies get programmed to remember what to do based on past experiences. Depending on whether those memories are happy or stressful, our bodies take the messages from our brains and turn them into chemicals in our bodies. Happy memories create oxytocin and the feel good hormone dopamine. Stressed, scary emotions create cortisol, the stress hormone. Once the experiences are over, our bodies remember that feeling and take the cues from our brain. It gets used to whatever our thoughts are and wants more of it- even if it is a stressful, negative experience!

It doesn't make sense that our bodies would be programmed to want more of the negative hormones, but if that is what we feed our bodies, it is exactly what happens. Our bodies like routine and patterns so therefore it is looking for more of what it already knows. If we try to change that from a negative to a positive experience, our body doesn't know what to do. It actually "feels" weird and might even feel like a bit of anxiety! Your body doesn't know what to do with this new energy and your brain might try to tell you to be worried.

I was raised with a negative mindset. Actually, I was in a toxic environment when I was young but I was being told "everything was fine". It's taken me years to move out of this. I realized that I didn't know how to be happy and I was scared of happy people. Immediately, my mind would tell me (this was an unconscious act) that I couldn't trust this person and that I better figure out what was wrong. My brain would look for evidence and wouldn't even know how to engage with happy people. Sounds crazy to those who know me, but it was true. I would put on a pretend happy face around the people and then go home and worry that I couldn't trust them.

When people are raised always looking for the good, it changes their brain and body chemistry. Since our brains are constantly searching for danger, a person who grows up in a negative environment has to retrain their brain so that life is viewed through a different lens-one that is searching for good things.

The problem is we hold onto our emotions for way too long and keep reliving the past experiences by talking about them over and over again. We stay stuck in those same emotions that were only supposed to last for ninety seconds!

Understanding our emotions is a complicated task- one that has to involve both our mind and our body. In Brene Brown's new book, *Atlas of the Heart,* she captures the complexity of understanding where our emotions come from, how our environment shapes our emotions and gives us the tools to move through our emotions, instead of burying them within ourselves. As Brown shares, "I want this book to be an atlas for all of us, because I believe that, with an adventurous heart and the right maps, we can travel anywhere and never fear losing ourselves."

We feel with our hearts, then our brains receive the messages and then we respond or act. At heartmath.org, it is noted that actually it is our heart sending messages to our brain. "Our heart rhythms affect the brain's ability to process information. The heart has 40,000 sensory neurons involved in relaying ascending information to the brain." If we think about this, then it is actually our emotional response that is cueing our brains to function. It is important to understand how our hearts can turn to love instead of fear. This then sends different messages to our brains!

This invisible world of energy connects us at a cellular level that is difficult to understand. When we stay stuck in victim mode and complain about how awful the world is, more of that appears because our body is accustomed to the feelings and the chemicals floating around in our blood stream.

Our brains are like a security system, constantly looking for danger. We theorize about this and then look for evidence to support our ideas. There are so many invisible inputs of information that go into this experience. Beyond what the physical eyes see, or our ears hear, our intuitive self is receiving messages to inform us about any and all events. For years, I shut this part of me off because I didn't understand how to listen to these signals. My brain was constantly looking for evidence instead of listening to messages from my body.

The only way out of negativity is to work on our body system- to make it feel good from within, an energetic feeling that is done with body regulation techniques like EFT (emotional freedom technique), yoga, breathing exercises, cold showers, exercise, EMDR (eye movement desensitization reprogramming), and many others. The list is endless but important to practice everyday.

I have many things on my bathroom sink. I went to reach for the tube of toothpaste and imagined grabbing the wrong tube. Hair gel wouldn't work so well on my teeth! That's what it is like to get up in the morning with the wrong feelings in the morning. It's like brushing your teeth with hair gel. We have to choose the right feeling to feel good each and every day. We have to do the work to relax our minds in order to prepare for the day.

The other thing that I wish Jay, Donna and anyone else thinking about suicide knew was that you are not the thinking part of your brain. It's important to first observe that part of your brain, disconnect from it and then tell it to shut up! You may thank it kindly for trying to protect you and then rewrite the story that your mind might have created based on love and kindness.

I sort of remember my mother's voice as she shared, "Well, you know her son committed suicide." It wasn't in a caring way but had a more judgmental tone to her words. At the time, I would have no idea that years later, I would connect with this woman who was from my small hometown. We were both writing about death and our connection to Heaven.

Cathleen was always kind when I saw her around town. I was a bit younger than her so I wouldn't really know her. I definitely didn't know her son but I would hear about her through a mutual friend while working on this book.

Her son's suicide shattered her beyond belief. It was through his death that she began to learn how to allow herself to grieve and discover a different way to live. She first received the help she needed with therapists and a variety of modalities to help not only her mind heal but her body too. She is grateful now to help others. She still experiences deep sadness but also the magical connection she has with her son now is such a gift to her. She shared her journey in her book, *Shattered Together: A Mother's Journey From Grief to Belief. A Guide to Help You Through Sudden Loss.* Her story encompasses David Kessler's Sixth Stage of Grief- Finding Meaning, where they both agree that "Pain is inevitable but suffering is optional." ~David Kessler

Through her loss, she discovered living life a different way. She quit her corporate job and followed her trail of grief to help others, creating a program called Stepping Stone to Grief (https://cathleenelle.com/shattered-together/). Her life was shattered but within that space, she discovered a whole new way to live with her loss. Her program helps not only the person's mind but she uses specialized techniques to help the person's body to heal as we hold our grief within our bones.

When she needs guidance in her life, she reaches out to her son and asks for a sign. She is able to receive her sign almost immediately because she understands the many ways Heaven is able to communicate with us. Using a variety of intuitive, spiritual abilities, she sees numbers, hears messages and even feels her son nearby. Her willingness to share her story has helped hundreds of people who have experienced loss.

Cathleen reminds me of my Grandmother. My Grandmother was full of laughter, kindness and love. I'm not sure when my parents shared with me the story of my Great Grandfather, but when they did, I never forgot it. It made me wonder if this event changed my grandmother's life in such a way that it actually changed who she was at her core, just like Cathleen.

It was 1918. My Grandmother was about to graduate from Peoples Academy High School. She was valedictorian in a class of about twenty students. I don't know what she said in that speech, but her courage and strength are an inspiration to me. Her father killed himself the very day of her graduation speech. Yet, she stood in front of a small crowd of family and friends and spoke anyway. Is this why my Grandmother was never negative to anyone? Is this why she was full of life? Had she seen what negative thinking could do to a person? Did she know and understand the secrets that I was discovering now? Was she grateful to be alive? Did her pain change her in a way that only some understand?

I never spoke to my Grandmother about her father's death. Even though nobody stated it, in my family talking about death was a social taboo that I learned at a very young age. I'm sure that her father's death changed her life forever. Maybe her father's death taught her to live each day more alive than the previous, to think of others and appreciate everything she had.

I couldn't write a book in 2022-2023 without acknowledging the pandemic. It is forcing every single person to face and talk about death. The fears are constantly being shown on TV and we all have a choice to choose love or fear. The fear of the virus and other stresses have caused more overdose deaths than Covid deaths in our little state. This pandemic has affected everyone's mental health in ways that we may never understand.

With death knocking on everyone's front door through the fear of the pandemic, it's time to re-evaluate how we live.

It's Christmas morning and I have a choice to make today. It's a choice most likely my Grandmother made when she was only seventeen years old. My choice is to be present with the ones I love and to be filled with gratitude.

Do I miss past Christmas's when my children were young and the excitement of Santa was in the air? You bet. Now I sit by the Christmas tree enjoying my cup of coffee, I notice a few of the lights on the Christmas tree aren't working. It is odd that it is only a part of a string. As I think of my Grandmother, they suddenly turn on. Was this my Grandmother with me as I write? Yes, I believe so therefore it is true. I don't need validation from others and I feel my Grandmother's presence helping me make my choice today.

I do hope my Grandmother cried for the loss of her father. I do hope they honored him at a service. I know nothing about him other than this one fact. I imagine that whatever was bothering him was just too much for him at the time. I do believe that when someone leaves this world in this way, they may regret their decision. At the time, they felt there may not be another way. This is their soul lesson.

When I dusted off the images from when I was young, I saw my Grandmother happy every time I visited. She lived next door so it was an easy run across the field to her back door. As she opened the door to the kitchen, I would either be interested in the built-in toy drawer under her china cabinet or would look to see if she had any of my favorite cookies with the raspberry jelly in the middle. The bible next to her chair was filled with notes and her diary sat there ready for her pen. I didn't really pay any attention to them when I was young; but we would find them years later. Her smile when I walked into her house was like a laser beam of light shining right into my heart.

My choice today is the choice I imagine my Grandmother chose all those years ago. I choose to be filled with love and kindness. I choose to embrace the memory of my Grandmother through being like her. I feel that is the best way to honor her memory, her legacy living on within me.

It can be easy during the holidays to miss the people who used to be here with us. When I am stuck in my grief, I have learned to turn toward Heaven and ask for help. I like to talk about the people who have passed and share stories about them. When I'm struggling in my life with a decision, I ask my Grandmother or my father for their help. I wonder what they might have done. I live my life encompassing the best qualities of who they were, allowing their legacy to continue on.

Also while working on this book, I had two friends who phoned me to reach out for help. Their exact words were, "I'm having dark thoughts of ending my life." (Please, if you or anyone you know are having these thoughts, reach out for help at https://suicidepreventionlifeline.org/) I know as a trained educator, the first question to ask someone who states this is, "Do you have a plan?" Then the next step is to make sure they get professional help, immediately if they do have a plan. They called me because they knew they didn't want to end their life. Neither of them were even close to developing a plan but just said they felt, "off". The first thing I told them was, "You are loved." I wanted both of them to feel love from deep within their hearts.

I can relate to this feeling of wanting to leave earth because through-out different periods of my life I have thought those same things myself. I used to beat myself up about the mistakes I made in my life and had difficulty letting go of the past. When these two people called me, they explained over and over all of the things wrong with their life. I listened and continued to say, "You are loved by many."

Then, when they were done sharing, I slowly guided them to think about what they did want. They were very caught up in what they didn't want, but what exactly did they want in their life? They were doing what anyone should do when having these thoughts, they reached out for help and for that I am grateful. This can be a difficult thing for many of us, but they did it. There was a deep trust and love with these two friends and although I am not a counselor, we worked through some of their negative thinking in a very different way than what they were used to.

Love from God/Universe/Spirit (whatever word you might use for something beyond what the eyes can see) is always there and loves each and every one of us. They slowly began to feel it and started to move their way of living toward a different style- one where they were able to feel joy and happiness instead of all anger and sadness. They were able to move past their mistakes in their life and understand that it was the behavior that was the mistake, not them. They were not a mistake. They were human and humans make mistakes. They didn't internalize the mistake and say, "I am bad". Instead they said, "I made a poor choice." They also stopped listening to that other voice inside their head- the one that is looking at life through a negative lens to keep us safe.

Did they heal overnight? Absolutely not. They began to slowly see that asking for help and then showing gratitude began producing small signs of magic all around them. Both were going through a breakup and this brought up feelings of deep pain and loneliness. They both were eager to move away from this deep pain to experience life fully.

Once they were able to feel the love, I asked them what they wanted in their life. They were so focused on complaining about how awful their life was it was actually creating more of those events. And, since their brain and body were used to that, it was a comfortable feeling for them. They were moulding their reality with their thoughts so more negative things kept showing up because that is what they were focused on.

Both of them shared about the anger and arguments they had with their significant other. I asked them if there was any grief within that anger. Anger is the easiest emotion because it hides all of the other emotions. Were they sad? Were they losing something they didn't want to lose? This was a turning point in their understanding of living differently. Both of them started reorganizing their thoughts with love and began to see the blessings each and every day; even though they were still losing their partners. It was grief in a whole different way. It was like a part of them was dying.

I received a text message that said, "I am finding at least about three coins a day. What does that mean?"

My response was, "You are loved and supported. Check the years. When you find them, ask the coins what you need to know right now. Trust your intuition. The answers are within you."

Finding the coins was more than just being a tiny bit richer. The coin was connecting them to a positive energy. The coins were my sign so that is what the universe used to give them a sign. It would be a way to get their attention.

"I keep seeing repeating numbers all day long. What does that mean?" Again I repeated, "You are loved and it is important for you to love yourself first." I encouraged him to google the different numbers to see what they meant. Each number was filled with more and more guidance towards a positive way to live.

"Monica, you are never going to believe this! I started my day with a mediation and gratitude practice. I felt so happy inside. I realized that I wasn't used to this feeling. I realized that there is nothing I can do about the past. I can apologize but I'm not going to stay in that bad feeling. It is so incredibly good to feel free! I have a different understanding of God now. I know he wants me to be happy and that it is okay to be happy. Even though I'm having a few bad days here and there, I'm not getting so upset about it. I'm observing my life like I'm watching a movie. I'm not attaching my self worth to the events that happen. I realize now I was so caught up in the negative and I talked about it all of the time- no wonder I kept manifesting more negative! I now want to talk about love and how the mind processes information and events. I want to meditate and clear my body to experience more love and I know that if anything shows up that is negative, it is like a test in school. I have to reorganize my thoughts back to love! This is so much fun! I am so thankful to have learned to live this way! I can't believe that I had no idea how to do this before. It would be great for everyone to know about this! Oh my goodness. I just feel so good inside! I am so excited to learn more about how to feel good. Thank you, Monica, for our connection and not judging me," Darcie's energy had seriously moved up the scale of vibrational energy and she was toward the top- with such gratitude that it bubbled up inside her. She had reached out for help, experienced deep gratitude and now was experiencing the life that is available to everyone.

It is through our pain where we find meaning in our life. Through their pain and darkness, they were both realizing that they had control of their thoughts. Our brains love patterns and even though it doesn't make sense that it would create more negative when we think negative, that's exactly what happens. Patterns make us feel comfortable. When they tried a different way, it was actually more difficult than staying the same. They were able to step back and observe the pattern and then change their thoughts. They "watched" their brain instead of "being" their brain. They were able to begin slow bits of gratitude and when their mind went to a bad place, they turned it around and remembered love. They both got new jobs with more pay. Talk about changing their life! They attracted exactly what they wanted with this new feeling.

A patterned belief was uncovered when I was talking with these two friends. We grew up in the 1980's, where college was pushed onto students. It was considered the only way to success. Is this still being taught in schools today?

Darcie was fifty-three and never felt that she had the career she dreamed of as a high school student. She felt like a failure so she kept pushing herself and wanted to enroll in classes to be a psychologist. I always encourage people to follow their dreams, but this dream seemed like it would put Darcie further into debt and wasn't really the best option for her at this time in her life. I got the feeling she would never feel complete until she finished the dream that began when she was young. By doing this, would she only be able to feel success based on society's definition of success?

"All I do is clean houses. I never really had a career," her voice oozed with regret.

"Why is cleaning houses a bad job? Why do you need a 'career'?" I asked. I suggested something different. People love to have someone clean their house and it is a good paying job. If she was good at it, why shouldn't she do it? Could she find joy within the job she has now? As I had often done, Darcie was living the life with the ideas of happiness being something that we chase, "We will be happy when... fill in the blank." I wanted Darcie to experience joy and love right now.

Darcie slowly let go of the expectations she had placed on herself so many years ago and re-imagined her life. She began listening to online trainings while cleaning and she began to find incredible magic in each day. She learned to love and accept herself just as she is right now. She sees joy in each day. Her thoughts about death taught her how to live differently and she was so grateful for the changes she made in her life.

Did both of them get the love of their life back? Well, that depends. They might not have gotten their romantic love but they sure as hell know how to love themself more. That is the most important soul lesson we can all learn. Self-love can cure anything.

"Be the best me that I can be." is my new motto and they both embraced it. I hope they always know how much they are loved.

I spoke at my Grandmother and my father's funerals. It was an honor for me to share memories and my love for them. My memories fill my heart with love and their legacy continues on.

Now, I live each day thinking about what people might say at my funeral. What do I want to be remembered for? What do I do each and every day that would be nice? I'm not talking about my job- although teaching was such a big part of my life. I'm not talking about the books I have written. Who am I each and every day? What am I like when things go well? What am I like when things don't go so well? How do I support other people? What do I truly care about?

When we are willing to zoom out the camera lens and look at our life from a different perspective, we get a clearer picture of who we are. When we don't get caught up in the stories and drama of life, that's when we see the real person in the mirror. From the outside looking in, I am able to give myself better advice each and every day.

My Grandmother ended every prayer at the dinner table with, "And let us be ever mindful of the needs of others." As a child, I had no idea what she meant by this. I'm sure she had seen a lot happen in her ninety-eight years. Now, even at fifty-four, I understand the importance of this.

Complaining about the pile of shoes in the mudroom? I'm glad the shoes are there because that means my kids are home. I think of the parents who have lost their children or the woman who wanted to be a Mom but was never able to conceive.

Complaining about taking the garbage out? I'm glad that I get to go for a walk outside. I'm happy that I have a garbage man who comes to pick up the trash each week.

Worried about money? I'm happy that I had the money to pay the bills or buy a coffee or buy gas for my car. I've got clothes that I am wearing and a house to live in.

Worried about tomorrow? I'll pray for a good outcome for wherever the road leads me.

Got stuck at a red light and running late? Maybe God was slowing me down or helping me avoid a car crash up ahead on the road.

Missing my Grandmother on Christmas day? I'll be a smiling and a happy Grandma to my own Grandchildren, filling their hearts with love just like my Grandmother did for me.

It's only through the pain that I am able to reframe my life. It's only through the pain of watching a mother lose her child that I view those shoes in the mudroom through different eyes. It's only through the pain of watching my own brother addicted to drugs and penniless that I feel rich when I am able to buy a cup of coffee. It's only through the pain of watching a car accident and seeing the person dead that I can pray for a safe trip every time my family and I travel. It's only through the pain of losing so many people in my life that I am able to find joy in each day that I am alive.

I'll be that person with an open heart who cares for everyone, just like my Grandmother because that is what this world needs. Because I didn't know that Donna and Jay were in pain, I'll be that person that brings light to others. It might only take one person's love to help someone feel better and change their life to be full of gratitude. I choose love.

Our hearts and minds are powerful things. What we feel, think and perceive determine our thoughts and the universe responds exactly to this.

Recently I was at a brunch where there were waffles with fruit and home- made whipped cream. Due to my medical diagnosis, gluten was a no-no for me. I knew that I couldn't eat the waffle, but I absolutely love whipped cream and blueberries. My heart, and stomach, really, really wanted them. My brain told me that people would think it was weird to just get the blueberries and cream. I spoke to my mind like I was talking with an old friend. I said it didn't matter what others thought- I was perfectly able to eat the blueberries and cream! It was like my brain was trying to convince me it wasn't a "safe" thing to do. I did it. I loaded the edge of my plate with berries and cream. As the whipped cream melted on my tongue and the berries burst open, a woman across the table said, "Are you eating just berries and cream?" I nodded and mumbled a "mm..hmm".

She then went on, "That is so awesome!" I then explained that I couldn't have the waffle but that I loved berries and cream. She was so excited for me and didn't judge me at all. She accepted me and I had made a conscious choice to do what I wanted. Life is like that- I choose to determine what I want and need and then do it. And, I was able to tell my brain that was riddled with fear to shut the hell up.

How we live is our choice. Understanding brain science helps us to make sure we are choosing our thoughts carefully. The invisible energy system that is running our subconscious is so powerful. It's important to tap into good energy each and every day. The universe is listening!

I choose to focus on the love that I had for the people who thought suicide was the only way out. I choose to acknowledge how they left this world, but not focus exclusively on the moment of their death. I want to also embrace who they were and continue their legacy. Their life was worth more than just that one moment.

**"Here's the hard truth: people who die by suicide don't die because of anything we did or didn't go. They died because they were mentally compromised, and their suffering mind told them that was the only way to escape excruciating pain. We can live our life in a way that honors them and brings hope to their struggle. All life has meaning, no matter how it comes to an end." ~David Kessler**

# 9

## Requesting a Sign from H(e)aven

"Open yourself to an encounter with heaven, be as a little child. Release your desire to the winds of the universe. Trust your angels to catch your wish and bring it to you in a delightfully surprising way." - Doreen Virtue

Haven was on her way home from college when she transitioned to the spirit world in a tragic car accident totaling the car and ending her life on earth instantly. Hannah, Haven's sister, would never see her again. It was Christmas break and her family couldn't wait for her to return from college. Penny, Haven's mother, shared with her closest friends that she had a sense that something was off that day. She wanted to pay for Haven's ride to the airport.

"I'm all set," Haven insisted. "My friend said she can drive me." Those words would replay in Penny's mind forever. I'm sure she always wonders- what if I had done something different? Was Haven's destiny pre-determined yet we think we have more control over our life and when we die?

Hannah became so distraught over the death of her sister, but when introduced to the idea of requesting a sign from Haven, she would forever transform her beliefs about signs from H(e)aven.

Haven's family lived in my husband's hometown, and she and Hannah were about the same age as my kids. I had never met Hannah, Penny, or Haven but heard the news of Haven's death through my husband. Even though I didn't know them, I felt the pit in my stomach and pain in my heart thinking about how sad this Christmas and every other day would be for their family.

Haven started getting my attention the week I began writing my first book, while I was vacationing on the gulf coast of Florida. Or, should I say, I started noticing more signs because I was more aware of this connection. My husband and I were driving to dinner when I spotted a hotel called "Beach Haven." Even though I had driven by it many times I had never noticed the name before and even when I noticed it this time, I had no idea that Hannah and Penny would eventually become a part of my life.

Just a month after noticing the hotel "Beach Haven," I met Penny at another of Rebecca's Messages from Heaven™ event. I attended the event with my sister who was close friends with one of Penny's friends. Penny seemed to have a whole team there to support her. She was sitting in front of me, a little to the left. When Rebecca walked over toward us, she was describing someone dying in a bad car accident. I knew Haven had transitioned in an accident, but so had my nephew, Tyler. More than one hundred eyes watched Rebecca to see what would happen next and who the message would be for.

Yes, I hoped with all my heart, Penny is going to get a message from Haven. I could feel her pain. Her grief, and everyone else's, was sitting in the room with us. It was in the air, invisible to the eyes but felt in everyone's heart. My best claire is clairsentience- being able to sense how people are feeling, especially if spirit is involved. It looked as if Penny might speak up. As she watched Rebecca moved closer, translating the messages from spirit. As she walked through the crowd to determine who the message was for. I wondered if Penny felt doubt creep into her mind. Was this woman who opened the night with the F word and had multiple tattoos really able to receive messages from dead people? I had been to many of Rebecca's events so I knew 100% that this lady was the real deal.

I felt jittery and excited and I was hoping Penny would make a motion to signal to Rebecca that the information she was receiving was connected to her daughter, Haven. Even a simple nod of her head would be enough for Rebecca to walk toward Penny. Penny was close to me but just far enough away so I couldn't give her a gentle elbow or kick her chair to encourage her to speak up.

Then Rebecca looked at me. When she asked me if I had a relative pass away in a car accident, I reluctantly nodded my head. My energy is so open that often Spirit brings messages to me. I could feel the audience's excitement as Rebecca asked me more questions. The energy in the room is such a mixed up feeling. There is sadness in missing our loved ones but also the room is so filled with love from everyone- both in Spirit form and those sitting waiting to connect to Heaven.

"Was it a relative who passed in the car crash?" Rebecca inquired.

"Yes," I replied, following the rules of not giving any more information.

"Was it a male figure?" My heart pounded and I started to tremble as tears filled my eyes remembering back to the shock of losing my dear nephew.

"Yes," I nodded my head, validating the information she gave.

"Are your families close? I get the feeling that you aren't that close to his family." Rebecca stated the information as if it was a fact, even though at first she asked me a question.

"True," I responded. "He lived in Tennessee so we didn't see them much." Tyler's death forever changed my life and the shock of his death sent me searching for purpose and meaning in my own life. I wouldn't even have been at this event if Tyler hadn't died so suddenly. Through processing my grief, I learned about signs that prove there is an afterlife, and that coincidences and synchronicities are planned by Spirit to guide us each and every day.

"He was young," she stated, not needing verification from me, but I shook my head anyway for her and the rest of the audience to know that I agreed. Twenty one years old is way too young to die. Tyler and Haven's time on earth was so short.

"You understand that his soul was taken from his body just before the crash, right? He didn't feel the pain of the impact. That's how it works when someone is in a car crash," she added the answer to her own question. "You see, we have a soul that lives in our physical body. When it is our time, the universe or God or whatever you want to call it, takes our soul back to the Spirit world so that we don't experience pain and suffering. He did not suffer. I want you to understand that." This was Tyler's message for me but I felt it was a dual message for Penny also.

I hoped it brought at least a little comfort to her.

"Are the two of you related?" Rebecca pointed to my sister sitting next to me. My clairsentience felt the shift in the energy in the room and I understood that another spirit was about to come through. The room was so quiet one would imagine that the people watching weren't even breathing. We were all anxiously waiting to see what Rebecca would say next.

"Yes, she is my sister, Debbie" I replied.

"She isn't related to the man who died in the crash. I feel like someone else is trying to come through now. This person is related to your sister too. Is your father in the spirit world?"

"Yes," I again went back to the yes or no response, not revealing any more information than needed for Rebecca to do her work.

"I'm seeing rose colored glasses. Did your father not have a sense of what was really happening in the family? Was he always thinking everything would be fine?"

There was no holding back our chuckle as Debbie and I responded in unison, "Yes." We both loved him dearly but sometimes he liked to view the world as always fine even if there was conflict.

Rebecca looked directly at me when she relayed the next message. "Okay, your father is sending a message that he loved you both very much. I don't want to hurt your feelings when I say the next thing. It wasn't that he didn't love you," she began, directing the comment at me, "but," she continued as she walked closer to my sister, "you were your dad's favorite. There was something about you that he especially liked. Did you work together? Was it like a family business?"

My heart was not crushed by her words as some might think. I know enough about Spirit to understand that there is only love and not any negative energy. Others might not react with the same human emotion that I did. I was thrilled for my sister. Debbie needed to hear that. Her relationship with our father during the last few years was strained and difficult. I thought maybe my sister wondered if he still loved her after all of those events.

My sister laughed through her happy tears and said, "Yes."

I'm sure the audience felt the love my father was sending to my sister through Rebecca and maybe even worried about my feelings. I wished I could explain that there is only love from the Spirit world. Nobody needed to worry about my feelings. Only love shines through to us all.

I wondered about Penny that night. Did Penny need to see this reading to open herself up to messages? I didn't speak to her that night and wouldn't for at least another year, after I shared my original dime story.

When people come into my life, I always know there is a lesson to learn. Sometimes it can be challenging lessons and other times it can be such an incredible positive connection that I am forever thankful to have them in my life. I believe each person teaches me something new. The more I shared my stories and felt the gratitude within me, the more Spirit began to connect with me. This would be true for Haven, even though I never knew her when she was alive.

Months after the event, Hannah and I would slowly begin to connect. My youngest son had started dating Hannah's best friend and Hannah married one of my sons' friends. Hannah moved to our small town about forty minutes away from her hometown. As our connection grew, Haven started showing up in my life more and more. A lot of times, her name showed up in books I read. Haven even showed up in a video about Major League Baseball pitcher David Price. In an interview with NESN that included a story about his friendship with Tyler, David said that baseball was always his "safe haven." The synchronistic events that connected the family and friends of two young people whose parents were from the same small town in Vermont dying in different car crashes seemed almost impossible to explain. Was Haven connecting with me so I would somehow be able to share my dime story with Penny and Hannah? Could my story help them believe in connecting with Haven?

When Spirit wants to get a message to someone, they will continually send messages over and over again. It's up to us to decipher the code with our intuition and our various spiritual senses.

While we were renting the camp on Lake Champlain, my son's girlfriend, Heather, noticed a book on the shelf. She said to me, "Check out this book. The author's name is Haven. I didn't know Haven, but sometimes it feels like she shows up. Do you think this could be a sign from her?"

"Yes! You are one of Hannah's best friends. Of course Haven would reach out to you! Especially since you are connected to me," I explained, so excited because my son's girlfriend believed in what my mother would have called "crazy" when I was Heather's age.

Recently, when I went in for a color and a cut, Hannah shared a story about a coincidence from H(e)aven. Someone suggested to her that she should do an experiment and ask for a sign from her sister. She didn't ask for just anything. She asked for something very specific. She didn't tell many people about her experiment but the results would surprise even a non-believer!

"I decided I would ask for the numbers 924. My sister Haven's birthday was on September 24th," Hannah explained.

I got all tingly inside my body just thinking about it. I felt such gratitude and love for Hannah sharing her story with me. The excitement of her story raised my energy level. My energy felt good even though the sadness of her loss was sitting like a thick, dark cloud in the room with us. I love sharing stories because it seemed to dissolve that sad cloud. Hannah would never be sharing this with me if I hadn't shared my dime story. I sat on the edge of my seat as I asked, "Did you see the number?" I knew numbers are a fun way to connect and they could show up on a sign, in a book or even the amount of a grocery bill.

"I wondered if it would be on a car license plate or the time on a clock or the number of something. I looked and looked for days everywhere I went. Then nothing happened. I wondered if this experiment was a bust. I mean, does this stuff really work?" Hannah laughed and maybe felt a bit silly because she already knew my answer to her question. She stopped cutting my hair; scissors and a comb in her hand. As our eyes locked in the mirror in front of me, I imagined both of us pausing wondering about how the Spirit world works. We both knew that sometimes there is no explanation for how coincidences and synchronicities happened and some have difficulty believing in such "weird" or "crazy" things. That is, until it happens to them.

There was this sense of peace as she continued on in her story and I reassured her that I obviously believe in signs. It's not like a ghost or a haunted spirit like some people might imagine. Signs from Spirit are like rays of sunshine filled with warmth, love and goodness.

"Well, I could tell you a lot of stories about dimes, numbers and other signs. Have you read my book yet? You are talking to the right person!" I laughed as she continued her story.

"I sort of forgot about it because nothing happened. Then one day I was cutting this young girl's hair. Her mother was sitting in the chair by the window. She looked like she was ready to give birth any day so I casually asked her when her baby was due. I couldn't even believe it and didn't know what to say. She told me she was due on September 24th. This woman was due on my sister's birthday. I couldn't say anything because she had no idea about my experiment. Isn't that crazy?" Hannah again stopped cutting my hair; absolute shock in her face while she was trying to rationalize how this coincidence could really happen.

"Oh my gosh. That is amazing!" I said almost as if speaking to Haven instead of Hannah. Her sense of humor shined down from Heaven. Over the last few months, Haven had been showing up in my life more and more. This was why. Haven tried to get me to talk to her sister. This was only the second time Hannah had cut my hair. The choice to switch hairdressers felt like a pull from a magnet inside me. My intuition guided me to Hannah but I knew Haven brought us together.

The thing about signs is that we can ask our loved ones for a sign but spirit decides how and when the sign will appear. Hannah received her sign from her sister but she wasn't done. There was more. I couldn't imagine what could top that story but I could hear in her voice that whatever happened next was going to be even more unbelievable and even crazier than the woman due on her sister's birthday. As I waited patiently for her to finish like a grand finale at the fourth of July, I felt like I was on top of the mountain when I found my first dime. Hannah was being "dimed" but it wasn't with a dime; it was a clear message through her requested birthday numbers.

"Then, days later," Hannah continued on, "I was so surprised that I was telling this story to another client of mine. When I did, the woman said suddenly, 'Wait, what did you just say? September 24th? My birthday is on September 24th.'"

"That's crazy!" I said, "Not only the number but two birthdays on the same day as your sister! That was her. Loud and clear. I hope you believe now!"

This message was an amazing synchronicity from her sister and Hannah knew it. The coincidence proved Hannah and Haven's connection was continuing on even after Haven's death. It was a different relationship but Haven was there anytime Hannah wanted to reach out to her.

I wrote my first book for people like Hannah. She and her family grieve every single day for their beloved Haven. They miss her so much it hurts. When Hannah shared her story with me, she glowed. Her sister's energy filled the room with love and light.

Hannah is listening to her intuition like never before and understanding how to live in a whole new way. This will forever change how she lives, how her family lives, and she will pass this on to the next generation. She won't have to wait to talk about signs from Heaven until she is fifty like me!

As I waited in the chair for my hair to dry, Hannah walked over toward the desk area. She laughed and said, "Well, guess what I just found?"

I turned my head and watched her bend down to pick something off the wood floor.

"What?" I asked.

"A dime," she answered. "It wasn't there when you walked in, was it?"

"Nope, I didn't see it and I have a pretty good eye for spotting dimes." I chuckled because we both knew if there was a dime to be found, I would be the one to find it. The dime was like icing on the cake after Hannah's story.

My haircut was finished and I met Hannah at the counter to pay. As I handed her my debit card, I spotted a ceramic container on the left side of the dark wooden counter. It had the words "change is good" written in black lettering. It was a place to leave a coin for others or take a coin if you needed one. There was a lonely dime sitting in it. Hannah was changing her reality and changing the way she lived her life. Change is most definitely good.

I hoped Hannah would always know that her sister, Haven, is with her every single day. Then, now, and forever, she is smiling down on Hannah's children. Haven is always with her mom and dad, too. It's a different way to be, but she is always there in the rainbow they see, the dragonfly that lands on their picnic table, or in the penny or dime they find.

Since sharing this story, I have connected with Penny and I am amazed at how these stories help all of us heal and feel closer to our loved ones. My grief for my parents was vastly different than losing a child. Dimes aren't necessarily their sign from Haven. Penny believes that Haven shows up in pennies because of her name, Penny! What a beautiful thing. Penny forever misses her lovely daughter. I hope she always talks about her. Their love forever connects them to Haven.

I am so grateful to Hannah and Penny for allowing me to share their story. I offered both of them a free Angel card reading as a thank you. When I did Penny's reading, the card she received was, "It had to happen this way." That was a very difficult card for me to share with her and I wasn't sure how she would respond. Life doesn't seem fair when we lose a young person. Some people believe that our death, just like our birth, is predetermined by a universal intelligence. Some souls are only here for a short time and many lessons are learned by the ones left behind. Through the pain, we all learn to live differently. Penny accepted the card with tears flowing and a knowing that this was true.

After I posted a blog about this incredible story, a friend posted on Facebook, "Haven is going to be a great plase to be." Kevin has difficulty spelling words correctly and his misspelling of the word Heaven meant the world to Penny, Hannah, and me. Haven seemed happy to send all of us a message. After I shared the screenshot of Kevin's comment, Penny shared a picture of the words written in the sandy beach, "Haven is in Heaven."

Hannah tried her first experiment with the spirit communication system. She wanted to see if her thoughts would actually create an experience that would show her that her sister was able to send messages. Finding success meant Hannah could begin to connect to her intuition and understand how her thoughts create her reality. The truth is, our reality is shaped by our thoughts and we are able to affect some of the outcomes through focus and intention. This can be applied to all areas of our life, not just spiritual connections with Heaven. Hannah was only beginning to understand how powerful this can be in our daily life.

Are you ready to conduct your experiment like Hannah? What will you ask for? Be specific. Choose something meaningful to you and the person you want to connect with. Dimes were significant to me because my dad gave me a special dime from his antique coin collection. Would you want a butterfly? A dragonfly? Another animal? What about a special number? Did you and your loved one have an inside joke that only you two would understand? Did they like the circus? Maybe ask for a clown or a circus tent. I've heard stories of people asking for oranges, nickels or even a certain car. It doesn't matter what you choose as long as you are specific.

I compare asking for a sign from Spirit to a filter when you are looking for something online. When I go shopping online for clothes, I don't just say, "I want some clothes." What exactly do I want? Do I want pants? A skirt? A shirt? What color do I want? What style do I want? Don't just ask for any sign because then you might not really be sure or believe. You might doubt the synchronicity if it is too general.

The more specific the request, the better you are able to believe the sign because it will be such an incredible coincidence if you receive it. If you want a butterfly, what color butterfly do you want? Hannah didn't just ask for numbers, she specifically asked for her sister's birthday. Just like a filter on a computer, filter your request so that Spirit is able to show you without a doubt that it is a sign from your loved one.

The comfort that we find in signs and synchronicities helps us see another way to view simple coincidences. Learning to recognize when Spirit may be sending you messages is like taking a key and opening a new door- except it is invisible and we can't see it.

Recently, Penny held a "Compassionate friends global candle lighting" on the anniversary of Haven's passing. I read it and wondered about Haven. A few hours later, I felt Haven's presence through a Facebook advertisement showing a picture of six colorfully striped birthday candles. Underneath the picture, the following message was written: "34 cozy gifts that turn homes into havens all under $50." Haven is such a cool name because the word is also used as a noun to mean a place of safety. Whenever I see the word Haven, it reminds me that H(e)aven is a safe place.

I sent the candle picture to Penny and asked her, "Did you post something about candles?"

"Yes! Always here with us!" she responded. Penny and Hannah's dear sweet Haven is right here.

Directions to request a sign:

1. Think of something that directly connects you and your loved one. Be specific.

2. Think about it for a long time and write it down somewhere. Feel the love in your heart for your loved one.

3. Look everywhere for the item. If you are looking for a number, it might be on a license plate or on the odometer of your car. If you are looking for an item like a butterfly and it is the middle of winter, look on your computer or decorations wherever you go.

4. Let go and allow the universe to be in charge. Awareness is the key to discover the magic of this type of communication. When you have faith that it works, miraculous coincidences and synchronicities happen!

When I began this journey of learning and writing about death, I didn't know just how powerful our thoughts could be. We are able to connect to Heaven with our thoughts- what a gift from H(e)aven.

# 10

## Invisible Energy

"Some people could be given an entire field of roses and only see the thorns in it. Others could be given a single weed and only see the wildflower in it. Perception is a key component to gratitude. And gratitude is a key component to joy." ~Amy Weatherly

What do you think of when you hear the word dandelions? Some consider it a weed while others think dandelions are beautiful. Imagine a field of yellow dandelions in a green bed of fresh spring grass. A young child views it as a pretty flower because they haven't learned yet what other people might tell them. That's what reframing is like. We view something totally different than the way we may have been taught. To many, picking up a dime meant they had an extra ten cents. My dimes are priceless to me because they connect me to a world we cannot see, hear, touch or smell. It's our perception that determines our view of life and death and whether or not we believe in an afterlife.

"And the dandelion does not stop growing, because it is told it is a weed. The dandelion does not care what others see. It says, 'One day, they'll be making wishes upon me.'" ~B. Atkinson

When my mother died, I went into caretaker mode. My father took a bad fall the very next day and since we had always been worried about my Dad's health, it was even worse now that he was grieving for his wife of almost sixty years. My father had little knowledge of the afterlife at the time of my mother's death so this time was a very challenging time for him.

I can still hear the musical tune to the show Grey's Anatomy replay like a broken record in my head, over and over and over again. It's a sound that brings me back in time. When I cared for my dad, I envisioned I would be able to function like I always had. Even though I had taken a family medical leave of absence from my new teaching job, I thought I would be able to plan my lessons for when I returned to school in April. Between all of the paperwork from my mother's death, caring twenty-four/seven for my father and dealing with my emotions, I could barely function. Instead, I watched episode after episode of Grey's Anatomy and Private Practice. So many episodes that I went through all of the seasons of each show. My brain was trying to escape from the reality of losing my mom and eventually it wouldn't be long until my dad was gone too.

My battery was empty because I didn't take care of my needs. I only thought about my dad. I couldn't focus on anything else and didn't really care much about my job or what was happening in the world. My world revolved around being with my father and trying to make sure his needs were met and to prepare his estate for when he transitioned to spirit.

Eventually I went back to work but still had to manage my father's care. I hadn't even truly processed my mother's death because I was too busy. The connection to my mother was basically nonexistent because I didn't have the energy to tune into the love in Heaven. It wasn't until my father died eight months later that my grief for both of them was so intense that I felt like a train had hit me square in the chest. The tears I cried for losing both of them came hard and fast. The monumental grief was deep and filled with a love for both of them. Even though I am about to tell you about positive energy within your body, know that I believe it is critical to allow deep grief to flow though your body and out your eyes. It's within that pain that I was able to remind myself of the love that I had for both of my parents and everything they had given me.

It's in our perception that we are able to find the key to opening a door to connect us to this other invisible world. A world that I felt as a child but now have come to understand more and more.

**"When you want something different for yourself, you have to start moving differently. Old keys don't unlock new doors." Unknown author**

I have found so many random dimes throughout the years. I wish I had started to count them. There have been so many! Some of these are so crazy that at times I wonder how these ever could have happened! In the show *BlackList*, there was a special coin that would be the "key" to the mystery. The coin was a Liberty Head dime. This particular day had been a rather difficult day at work and I know that this coincidence was a sign to hang in there.

It's only in looking back that now I am able to see that the universe was supporting me in ways that I would have no idea or that would have no explanation.

Now, there are so many dimes, numbers, heart shaped rocks and other signs that it is a challenge to keep track of them all. I am extremely grateful for each one and they have changed the way I live my life.

The universe is so amazing and powerful- more than we can even imagine. When we write down our dreams and goals, the universe listens but makes it even better than we could ever imagine.

There are seemingly small changes to the way I learned how to mold my reality with my thoughts.

Let's follow the thought process through an example. Wording is the key to unlock the doors to Heaven and living a more spiritual life.

Let's go back to the example of a sign from my father and walk through some of the blocks that might be blocking a person's connection. Let's say that I tried this phrase when I sent my request for a sign:

• I really really hope that I will receive a sign from my Dad.

MONICA L MORRISSEY

Do you hear the desperation in this? I hear people say all the time, "I've never gotten a sign." I reply, "Yup, and you won't until you stop saying that." This is actually sending the wrong signal to the universe. This is created out of a lack of something. The universe hears lack of abundance and the absence of something, so it sends more of that.

This intention also comes from the sign being in the future. Since today is the only thing we are able to experience, then writing something that happens in the future never comes because tomorrow is going to turn into today and then the next day is going to be tomorrow. Today is the present, both literally and figuratively-as a gift.

It is important to reword the request to be in the present moment-as if it has already happened. I felt it from within myself and didn't just think about it in my head.

• I am grateful for my signs from Heaven.

I felt it within my body and imagined that it already happened. Because I had experienced the feeling of the dime on the mountain, my body was in tune with this super excited feeling of connecting with Heaven. The universe is better able to deliver if we "fake it until we make it!" Sometimes when we try too hard we are trying to control the outcome. We have to let go and believe that it is happening right now.

The key to creating our reality with our thoughts is to open up the door to a much wider option. That way, the universe is able to make it even better than we ever imagined. Now, when I envision my life and the future, this is how I write:

• I am so very grateful and thankful for all of the dime signs because I love how my dad connects with me. I know he is here with me helping me write. I can hear his laugh as he chuckles every time he tells a story. I'm so thankful that he is still a big part of my life, even though he is no longer here physically- his legacy lives on within me.

Think of molding your reality like searching for something on Google. Google and Facebook track your actions (thoughts) by what you are clicking on. Then, it gives you more of what you want. The universe is the same way. What we think about then becomes true and the universe sends us more because it thinks we want more! For the person who keeps saying, "I never get signs," they will continue to never receive a sign. For the person who remembers the love of the person in Heaven and feels the love, then it is going to be easier to connect and receive signs.

Dimes and other signs from Heaven keep appearing in my life because I know what it feels like to receive them. I believe at a very deep level in this connection to where we have the ability to connect to this invisible world with all of our natural intuitive abilities. We all have this natural ability. We just have to spend time in a quiet space to access it.

I'm very grateful for all the people who are here today and for the people who passed. Now, when I think of my parents, I try to remember a good time that I had when they were alive. I love to remember their legacy and embody that in my life.

Signs can be sent in a variety of ways. The most common signs from loved ones include butterflies, coins, dragonflies, deer, ladybugs, repeating numbers, rainbows, feathers, electrical problems, or music. The sign might be on the license plate of a car, a street sign, a computer, or a sign on a wall. Your sign might be found on the total of a bill or the change from a purchase, or a cloud in the sky. It's a mystery how coincidences and synchronicities happen, but they certainly show us we are a part of something beyond the physical world and our human thoughts. Our loved ones want to show us they are still with us.

In order for the communication system to work, it is important for us to work on our bodily energy. This is why it is so important to process your grief in whatever way works for you and then to find gratitude each and every day. There are so many emotions when someone dies that it is impossible to understand them all. Whatever you feel, allow that feeling in. Acknowledge it and then work to release it. Thank the emotion for being there and then ask yourself what you need in that moment. Cry, scream, reach out to a friend, watch a movie, eat ice cream. Whatever you need to do, do it and be okay with it. Ask for help if you need it! When we allow ourselves to move through the feeling, then it is better able to release.

We have emotions to help us survive and learn. Since I never learned how to move through my emotions instead of getting stuck in them, I used to hold onto my emotions like a baby's security blanket. Each time we retell stories where we were hurt, our body and mind think the event is happening again. It's important to share the story but then let it go. It's in the past and when we keep bringing it into the present, our bodies respond with the same emotion over and over again. Emotions were only meant to last about ninety seconds to help us learn to survive. I learned how to move through the emotion and then be in the present moment- which is filled with amazing new moments.

Since our emotions are what drive our energy system, it is important to understand how our mind, body and soul are connected. Think of our energy system like a battery. Negative emotions drain the battery but positive emotions charge our battery. Gratitude is the highest form of emotion for charging our battery. Sadness and anger drain our battery. When a loved one dies, our energy system (or battery) may seem so low that we can't imagine life where it would ever be recharged. That's what happened to me all those months I sat watching episode after episode. I seemed to be stuck and had no idea how to move out of my emotions. I had not started a gratitude practice and didn't understand how that might help me. Our internal energy sends a vibrational frequency to the other side that either helps or hinders Spirits' ability to connect.

When a soul returns to Spirit form after leaving the physical body, his/her battery is fully charged and vibrating at a very high speed. We, in our human form, have to try to match that energy level. The more positive our thoughts are, the more we are able to connect. This is challenging to experience during a time of grief, but it is the only way to help the communication system work properly. Remembering the good times we had with our loved ones helps charge our battery, making it easier for them to connect. Even though I cried on top of that mountain the day I found that first dime, I was able to feel the love within my heart. My connection with my father was strong and he was there with me.

Positive and negative emotional charges are exactly what you need to know and understand if you want to receive messages. Think of a time when you were so excited that you were able to feel it inside of you. Whenever I told my dime story, it seemed like my bones were plugged into an outlet because my body was so excited. Others reported feeling a "buzzing" in their body or like water trickling through their body. This is the energy to connect with. Now, remember a time when you were upset, sad or angry. For me, because I hate being lied to, when someone tells me something that I know is not true, I get triggered and inside I feel very angry. Feel both of the positive and negative feelings and then make a commitment to focus on the good feelings, especially love. That perspective helps to connect and open the door.

How do you do that? Think of the good times you had with your loved one. Remember who they were as a person. Maybe even write a letter to them. Pretend you are talking to them. What would they say to you? How would they want you to live? All of these help bring them closer to you.

Especially notice how the good feeling feels. I realized that because of past traumatic events that happened in my life, I was actually scared of this happy feeling. Anytime I felt happy, I worried that something bad was about to happen. I had intense anxiety anytime something happened or I traveled. I was afraid of everything! I had to train my mind to tell my body that everything was okay and it was good to have this feeling. Our bodies were built to remember negative events to keep us safe. Originally, humans needed to make sure to run away from lions and tigers and bears. Nowadays, we don't need this as much, but it is still a part of our human system. Our minds worry constantly that something bad might happen again. It's up to us to repattern our minds to live in gratitude and tell ourselves that we are safe and okay.

The chakras are invisible energetic centers in your body that affect our emotional and physical well-being. The ideas about chakras date back to 1500 BC and originated in India. Nowadays, the understanding of chakras has spread to the Western world, especially in Yoga and Reiki healing.

There are seven chakras and they go from the root chakra (base of your spine) all the way to your crown chakra (the top of your head). Each one is responsible for different emotions, which, in turn, affect our physical body. When chakras are aligned, the physical body is well and healthy. When a chakra is blocked or out of balance, this may lead to health or emotional issues.

Ancient scriptures relay that the chakras are like a sphere or ball. We have to use our imagination to sense the energy. During a Reiki session, the practitioner may envision the chakra of the client to help remove blockages and re-align the client's energy. Many yoga sessions are focused on aligning chakras.

Each of the seven chakra centers of the body correlate to a color, an element, a variety of emotions, a specific area of the physical body and specific areas of physical health. Here is a quick reference:

| Chakra | color | element | location | emotions | Physical manifestation |
|--------|-------|---------|----------|----------|------------------------|
| Root | red | Earth | Base of spine | Survival, stability, self-sufficiency, security, fear, confidence, finances | Arthritis, constipation, bladder, colon |

| | | | | | |
|---|---|---|---|---|---|
| Sacral | orange | Water | Lower abdomen | Sexuality, creativity, self-worth, compassion, intuition | UTI's, low back pain |
| Solar Plexus | yellow | Fire | Between navel and rib cage | Ego, anger, aggression, self-esteem, confidence, focus | Digestion, liver, diabetes |
| Heart | green | air | Heart region | Love, attachment, compassion, trust, passion caring optimism | Heart problems, asthma, weight |
| Throat | blue | space | Base of throat | Inspiration, self-expression, creativity, communicating, faith | Sore throat, |
| Third eye | Indigo | none | In-between eyebrows | Intuition, spiritual connection, self-knowledge | Headaches, blurry vision, eye strain |

| Crown | violet/ white | none | Top of head | Spirituality, enlightenment, dynamic thought and energy | Depression, anxiety |
|---|---|---|---|---|---|

Now, when your battery is fully charged, your chakras are aligned and you are grounded, it is time to get in touch with your intuitive gifts. These gifts were given to everyone at birth and they help us connect to the spiritual world. In Kindergarten, everyone learns about the five senses: hearing, sight, taste, smell and touch. What we don't learn in public school is the spiritual senses. These are called our "Claire" abilities and they mimic the senses but they are invisible and are part of our spiritual being, where our intuition is able to send us messages.

There are five main claires; clairvoyance, clairsentience, clairaudience, clairtancy and clairgustance. Each one taps into a different energetic way to receive messages from invisible thoughts, actions and coincidences. A person uses their five senses to tap into this energetic system to increase their intuitive abilities. Just like a cell phone works on top of a mountain; your senses are able to receive messages like radio waves traveling across time and space.

We are born with these heightened senses but as we grow older we tend to forget them, especially if they are not encouraged. Each person is gifted with at least one or more and some work better than others. It's through these senses that our loved ones are able to send messages.

Clairvoyance is clear seeing. When I was a young child, I had the ability to see entities floating around. They were like bubbles of white light. Some people actually see the shapes of people. Sometimes instead of seeing it in physical form, a person sees the vision in their mind. They may receive intuitive guidance about what is going to happen or may feel like they had a deja vu experience, where they feel like they have been here before. Dreams are another way to receive messages through clairvoyance abilities.

Clairsalience is receiving messages through a scent. Even though there seems to be no physical evidence, the person may smell roses that might remind a person of their Grandmother or even cigar smoke to remind them of an Uncle or Grandfather. Nobody else in the room smells what the person smells but the person knows they are able to smell it.

Clairaudience is the ability to hear even when it seems nobody is talking. For me, it is someone whispering to me but other people may hear voices or sounds that seem real. At times, people may think they are going crazy if they don't understand their gift because nobody else hears what they are hearing.

Clairtancy is when people receive intuitive guidance through touch. They don't need to have a physical object near them but they sense how the object feels to understand the message.

Clairgustance is receiving intuitive guidance through your sense of taste. A particular flavor may remind a person of an event that happened. Or, a person may get the taste of alcohol or medicine. Alcohol could be a clue the person liked to drink and medicine could be a sign of sickness.

So, like the senses we learned in Kindergarten, there are the following Spiritual senses that relate to the five senses.

**Sight- Clairvoyance**
**Smell- Clairsentience**
**Hearing- Clairaudience**
**Touch- Clairtancy**
**Taste- Clairgustance**

Beyond these claires, there are two more that have more to do with emotions. They are claircognizance and clairsentience and are related to the third chakra (solar plexus) and the fifth chakra (heart chakra).

Claircognizance is the gut feeling deep in your soul, where "You know". It isn't your brain rationalizing and convincing you of something. It is your whole body sending you a message. It can come from your gut or your heart and it is often this deep knowing that you have difficulty explaining to others. For instance, someone might know that something is going to happen in the future; either good or bad. My friend Kevin has the ability to guess when someone is about to have a baby. He even told my son, "You are having a baby." Kevin had no real reason for knowing this but said it matter of factly. It was true but my son and his girlfriend had just found out and hadn't told anyone yet. My son shared this with me and said, "How the heck did he know? We hadn't told anyone yet!" My son was so shocked he didn't know how to respond because Kevin was right.

Clairsentience is the ability to feel the emotions of others and it is by far my best claire. I am able to sense energy in the air. Obviously, we can't "see" an argument in the air floating between people, but if I walk into a room where there has been an argument, my senses alert me that there is tension. The same is true for when love is in the air!

Just like I wanted a sign from my father the universe heard and created that experience. Did my inspiration come from some sort of inner knowing that this was possible? The thought appeared out of nowhere. Could my intuitive self guided me during that moment and I wouldn't know it until I found the coins? The invisible world of communication is one of the greatest mysteries of our world.

All of these claires are our guidance system and our loved ones use these types of communication. We have to learn to decipher the messages. When I was young, I didn't understand how this worked and I tried to cover up my gifts. I had no way of knowing or understanding because I was born into a family system who didn't understand how any of this worked. For years, I either drank alcohol or ate food because it helped to dull these senses.

When I embraced my gifts and started writing, I began to understand how to live a more Spiritual life. Since we are souls with a body and not a body with a soul, it's important to connect back to our true selves. The events that transpired in my life were so amazing that I wanted to share them. When we allow the universe to work its magic, we may be surprised at how amazing this human journey can really be.

Within each story you hear how myself and others connect to someone who no longer has a physical body. Just by reading this book, your energy may be recharged and you may experience life in a whole new way - one in which you feel better and know how to turn to love instead of other emotions. For when we do this, our energy is ready with a fully charged battery and the universe is ready to shower us with blessings from Heaven.

# 11

## Help from Spirit

"Sometimes you get what you want. Other times, you get a lesson in patience, timing, alignment, empathy, compassion, faith, perseverance, resilience, humility, trust, meaning, awareness, resistance, purpose, clarity, grief, beauty, and life. Either way, you win."
~Brianna Wiest

My life changed the day my father died. Not in the way one might think. Yes, I was now without both of my parents. Yes, I had to deal with the estate and all the things that go with it. Yes, we needed to plan a funeral or a celebration of life- whatever we wanted to call it. Yes, we would never celebrate another holiday with them. Yes, I wouldn't be able to call my parents to see how they were doing. All of these things were true and they did change my life. The morning my father died, I changed one habit of mine to remind myself that I have the power to control my life and my thoughts.

On that day, I decided to drink my coffee without eating anything first. This may not seem like some big, major revelation, but for me it is always a reminder that I choose my thoughts and beliefs. I also have the power within me to change my life with my thoughts.

I tried to sleep for a few hours the last night when my father was alive. It was the third night I had been up all night helping to care for him. At 3:00AM, I got up to see how he was doing. I wanted coffee but I wasn't hungry. I decided to change a long time habit.

I love coffee but always told myself that I needed to have something in my stomach before I drank that first cup. Since that day, I start every morning with a cup of coffee and no food. I do this to prove a point and it has turned out to be the best part of my day. While drinking the coffee, I remind myself of all of the memories that are a part of me and I write ten gratitudes and five aspirations to start my day. Then, I either write or read for at least another half hour. This time to me is precious and I love to start my day like this. Each day that cup of coffee reminds me that I have the ability to change and reminds me how grateful I am to be alive.

Here are some of my gratitudes:

- I am grateful for the phone call from my friend because I value our friendship.
- I am grateful for the groceries I bought yesterday because we have food in the fridge and cupboards.
- I am grateful for a reader sending me a dime story because I know they are connecting with their loved ones.
- I am grateful for sliding with my Grandsons because we had so much fun making memories.

When I wrote my first book, the publicist focused on my "deep grief" of losing my father. This bothered me and I couldn't figure out why. When writing this book, I realized it is because when people think of grief, they immediately might be sad. The problem or disconnect I felt was that I was happy that I had this new relationship with my parents. I felt my parents supported me each and every day, more so than when they were here on earth. It was such a different experience for everyone else because they didn't have this deep connection with Heaven that I have. Yes, I was sad that my parents were no longer with us but they had a wonderful life and it felt like a normal part of life to say goodbye to them. I cried, asked for help and thanked God for the signs.

Life can throw us curve balls when we aren't paying attention or appreciating all that we have. This is true for me even though I've been doing this work for years. I wasn't ready for this next event in my life but it sure did teach me more about the quantum world that was so mysterious and elusive to me before. The invisible connection proved to me that we are all loved and supported in ways that are difficult to understand.

I lost the dime necklace my dad gave me. I felt more lost than when he died. Grief appeared suddenly and I wasn't sure how to handle it. It was grief for my missing necklace but it showed up like my Dad was dying all over again. I couldn't talk about this to anyone.

When I lost my dime and I was at a book event, I wasn't able to say, "My Dad gave me this dime from his coin collection," because I had to wear a decoy around my neck. The words were not true so I was unable to speak them. I replaced the dime I wore around my neck with one I bought at a coin store. It wasn't "the one" but it was a prop I could use when I wanted to talk about my books.

"My Dad gave me a special liberty head dime from his coin collection," I reworded my sentence to make it true as I grabbed the necklace around my neck. That's the best I could do right now. I couldn't lie and each time I said it I winced because inside I knew that I had actually misplaced the dime from my father. It was the dime that had started my entire spiritual journey.

How could a person who wrote two books about this special dime lose it? My energy was off and I felt like an imposter playing a role I wasn't fit to play. I felt I was a failure. I had not taken good care of my dime and now it was gone.

I know I put it "someplace special" where "I would always remember." I didn't want to talk about it to anyone and didn't for months. I kept praying that by some miracle I would find my dime. I believed in prayer and I knew this was a key part of my learning and growing. My prayers were very different than in the past. They included a feeling instead of begging for something. It wasn't, "God- please return my dime." It was more, "I'd love you to return my dime." I asked for the what and the when and how were up to Spirit.

Finally, I decided to share this news with a few people. I was lost and needed help. Maybe I just misplaced it or the cat had decided it was a great toy. I rummaged through clothes in my dresser drawers and looked under books, furniture or anything that might be covering it up. I wondered if I would ever find it. I checked a lot of "special spots" where I might have placed the dime. A drawer. Inside my father's antique clock. A special wooden bowl. Each place I looked, I seriously found a dime because I sprinkled my dimes in different places throughout my house. Just like the heart shaped rocks sprinkled all over the mountain, my house is filled with dimes and pennies.

I gave up but this weighed on me like I was carrying a fifty pound bag of rocks. I beat myself up about it. I had to face the fact that I lost it and I wasn't sure it was coming back. My grief came back and I missed my father. I remembered the good times with my parents. I remembered the moment my father said, as he woke up from his nap, "Hey. You know those dimes that were in that collection? Those different dimes? Could we have those made into necklaces?"

On March 14, 2021, I decided to write a request in my journal for my dime to be returned. This is what I wrote:

"I have a request. I would like you to return the dime you gave me from your coin collection. I understand that there was a deep lesson for me to learn when I lost it. I have been working on being more grounded and in the present moment. I also realize that although I am able to manifest some things in my life, ultimately Spirit helps guide me. I allow life to flow naturally. I am open to receiving abundance and I know that I am exactly where I need to be in life."

Organizing and cleaning my house helps me move my internal energy. Some people say that what our environment looks like is a reflection of our insides. As I redesigned myself, I redesigned my environment. I decided that I was going to redesign my work from home office to grow my card reading, Reiki and coaching business. My husband built me beautiful pine bookshelves to display all of my books. I love to read and my personal library grew each month to the point that I really needed a way to organize them.

As I was putting the books on my new shelves, I decided to open this one particular book. It was the book *The Astonishing Power of Emotions, Let Your Feelings Be Your Guide* by Esther and Jerry Hicks. Esther and Jerry write about how we create our world with our thoughts. They speak of our vibrational energy being alive and how to reprogram any negativity into positive affirmations.

My intuition guided me to open that book. I didn't open any other books that day.

The entire dime necklace fell out of that book. Tears came and I felt the weight on my shoulders release the guilt I had felt about losing my dime. When we let go of guilt, shame or other feelings that weigh us down, we offer a space in our hearts for love and connection.

That necklace then lived on my neck for weeks. My intuition told me, "Don't wear the necklace. You might lose it again." I didn't listen. I felt like I had my Superpower back and if I didn't have it on my neck, I wouldn't feel whole again. I decided to ignore that little voice warning me.

My head was looking down as I went to get up from my chiropractic adjustment. My necklace caught on the metal bars of the table but I released it quickly.

On my way home, I grabbed my necklace from beneath my sweater. Instead of being a closed circular rope around my neck, it was one long, unclasped string. At the moment my necklace was stuck in the table at the chiropractic office, it had broken the hook. This meant the dime didn't have anything to hang on to. I panicked. My dime was gone yet again. I started searching for the dime in my sweater, in my seat and all around me in the car.

I phoned the chiropractor and explained the situation to them. Would they mind looking for my dime? Would they please check the table, the room and the parking lot? I hated to call and ask them but

ONCE UPON A DIME

also was desperate to find my dime. I asked for help but they might not really understand the significance of this particular dime. It was worth way more than ten cents.

How could I let this happen? Why was this happening? Would the dime be lost forever this time?

My thoughts had come true. I had lost my dime yet again. Did I actually create my reality with my thoughts? I felt that it was my fault. I had only had the dime back for a few short weeks and this time, I wasn't sure if it would ever return.

I was devastated and my heart was broken. This time, I felt like I hadn't appreciated the dime enough. I had assumed that now that I had found it, I would always have it. And, I hadn't realized how much that the universe really listens to all of our thoughts.

When I shared this with my friend, Tracy, she laughed as she said, "Spirit gives and Spirit takes. It controls the dime. It knows when you need it." What? Is it possible that my father, who had technically "died", was able to somehow control events like this in my life? I had to be willing to think that something powerful was happening.

I felt it deep within me and was willing to learn some lessons with my loss. This is what I discovered when I lost my dime for the second time.

1. Appreciate everything you have each and every day. Even simple things like your morning coffee or your bed. Imagine life without these things and you are able to realize just how abundant your life truly is.
2. Slow down. I moved so fast when the necklace got stuck that I didn't notice it broke. If I had gone slower, I might have noticed the necklace was broken and found the dime right then and there.
3. Let go of attachment to physical objects. I won't find peace and happiness with the amount of things I have. Even though I had lost my superpower necklace, I actually had the superpower

within me all the time. I let go of the need for a physical object to remind me that Divine energy is within me.

4. Watch my thoughts. Because I had kept worrying about losing the dime, that is exactly what happened. I had seriously created my reality with my thoughts but not in a way that I wanted!

5. Spirit is in charge, not me. I had to let go and know that I am not able to control everything in my life. It's my job to have sincere gratitude for everything in my life and to know that God's plan for

   me is way better than I can even imagine.

6. It is okay to be okay where I am and not always searching for happiness in the next thing.

For days, which turned into weeks, which turned into months, I asked Spirit for my dime back. I scoured the parking lot every time I went to the chiropractor. I cleaned my car often, never daring to vacuum my car because I was afraid the vacuum would eat my dime and I would never get it back.

My faith was being tested. I prayed often and it went something like this: "Would you please send my dime back to me? I would really, really, really like it back. Thank you! Thank you! Thank you!"

I felt it deep within me that Spirit would eventually return my dime to me. As the months rolled on, my faith began to diminish.

That same summer, I attended the Psychic and Beyond Event in Connecticut hosted by Rebecca Ann Locicero. The weekend was spent doing intuitive readings, selling my books and speaking to a small crowd how my ideas about death changed since my father had died. I truly believe that when we die, our souls stay here on earth- invisible to the naked eye. Their souls are without their physical bodies- not like in the movies haunting people. They are here to love and support us. I believe we are able to connect with those who have transitioned to this other invisible dimension.

I then went on to explain how to ask for a sign and shared a story about my signs. During this session, there was a woman in the audience who I thought had grief radiating from her body. I could feel it in the air. I decided to end my speech a little earlier and ask if there were any questions. She raised her hand and began to tell me her story.

"My husband told me before he died that he would show signs to me in a waterfall," she shared and her anger poured out of her aura and spilled into the room. "I have been several times to the waterfall where he asked me to marry him. I get nothing every time I go there." Her words were filled with frustration, disappointment and disbelief that she would ever be able to receive a sign. I know what that felt like because I doubted this connection for so many years.

I felt that she was trying too hard and trying to control exactly when the sign would happen. I explained this to her and she seemed even angrier at me. I could tell she deeply missed her beloved husband. I wasn't sure there was anything that I could do for her other than share my own experiences so that maybe, if she was able to let go of the need to control, a sign may appear out of nowhere.

That's when it happened. A thought appeared in my head. I put my books down on the table nearby. I looked at her as I formed a heart with my hands. I told her that for some reason I keep hearing, "Show her a heart. Show her a heart."

"I keep seeing a big heart and he wants you to know that he loves you so much and that he is always with you," I said.

Instantaneously, the woman began crying. "I can't believe you just said that," she whispered through her tears. I knew there was more so I stayed quiet as our eyes locked. This gave her the space to share her story and for me to honor her grief.

"I was recently at the ocean with a friend of mine. I searched and searched for either a rock or a seashell in the shape of a heart. I didn't find any. I was so sad I couldn't even think straight. I kept thinking, 'Why won't he send me a sign?'. When my friend and I got back to our towels to sit down, she said, 'Look.' When I looked to where my friend was pointing, there was a heart shaped seashell right next to my towel."

The crowd responded with "oh my God" and "wow". I have no idea where the heart idea came from but I do know that the message was perfect timing for this woman. Spirit spoke to her when she let go of the need to control the outcome. She knew her husband was there and now she believed even more. May she always feel him near her.

I knew I had to let go of the need to control so that my dime would come back to me exactly when it was supposed to come back to me. Letting go is one of the most difficult things to do in this earthly life. I had to have faith and pray.

This book was partially written, but I didn't have a solid ending. My books are not something that I am able to plan ahead and write an outline for. This is a prescriptive writing process that does not work for me but since I was entering a contest to try to win a book contract with a large publishing agency, I tried to use the outline form suggested by my writing coach.

When trying to work with a publishing agency, an author writes a book proposal. For nonfiction, the book doesn't even need to be written. This writing process is great for some writers but I knew in my gut that I wasn't able to do it because my books are filled with stories from my life. My book proposal needs to be written after I write the book!

I worked with a writing coach to prepare that book proposal and am so grateful for the opportunity but inside I knew something was missing. I was writing to try to impress someone and it wasn't coming from my heart. Also, I couldn't figure out the ending. I had a lot of stories, but was missing a key part of understanding how this all works.

Anyone who has ever experienced grief knows that grief is not like a cold that you eventually get over. Grief is always present. It ebbs and flows like the waves in the ocean. Sometimes it is calm and other times it is stormy. It is always sitting inside your heart and walking right beside you everyday. Through losing my dime, I was again experiencing deep grief for my loss. The loss wasn't about the dime, it was about losing both of my parents. The dime was just the physical reminder.

What if there was a different way to experience grief? What if life was everlasting? What if the person wasn't actually gone? What if we were able to sense our loved ones all around us?

I wrote the book proposal with a theme about reframing grief. Honestly, it was a flop. It was a flop because I was writing to impress someone and I lost myself as a writer.

After finishing the book proposal, I walked away from my writing. I needed some time to just "be" instead of being busy all of the time. I let go of the outcome but inside my heart I knew that the book didn't have a good frame. I didn't even know the ending of the book. This was in March of 2021; exactly a month after I lost my dime for the second time.

Eldon, my father's best friend, passed away on June 18, 2021. His death inspired me to pick up my pen again. I wasn't able to plan the ending in my outline because the ending hadn't happened yet!

On July 13th of 2021, I decided it was time to write again. I was ready to write this book. I printed off the material I had so far and planned to work on it two days later.

That's when it happened. I changed my thinking. I decided to just be me and write however I wanted to write. I wanted this to come from my heart, not some prescribed writing outline. My stories are based on Spirit and energy, not the analytical part of my brain. I hadn't realized it before but trying to please others is what was blocking my writing. I let go and let Spirit help me.

My mailbox is located a quarter of a mile away from my house, at the bottom of a long, dirt driveway. As I drove a few feet past my mailbox on my way home from work, I parked my car. The radio blared Spiritual music as I left the car door open. I sang as I half danced, half walked to the mailbox. It was the day after I worked on my manuscript, I returned home from work to discover something so preposterous that I struggled to make sense of it.

There, amidst the stones and gravel, was my long lost dime.

Spirit sent me my dime at the exact time that I needed a gentle push to get back to my writing. I had learned yet another lesson; one that keeps showing up in my life. It was important to "Be the best me that I can be."

When I worked on my manuscript this time I was able to write in a different way. One where I wasn't trying to impress anyone and I was being authentic. I believe that my father knew and returned my dime to me as a sign of encouragement.

Spirit knows when the timing is right and when we need a sign. I had requested the what- "I would like my dime back" but the how and when had to be so unexpected that I would recognize the sign and receive the message.

For those who live in the country, they might understand why this was such a miracle because they know what happens to our dirt roads. For those who don't, I'll try to explain why finding this dime on my short path to my mailbox was such an improbable event.

When I lost my dime in February, it was the middle of winter in Vermont. This means that the road and driveway are plowed several times a week. The snow, along with the dirt are pushed around in every direction to clear the roads to drive.

Then, during March and April, the snow melts and the frost underneath the dirt pushes from beneath to cause up to one foot deep ruts in the mud that only a truck or an SUV are able to drive through. As the frost disappears, the water then soaks into the ground and the dirt is smooth again. Mud season is Vermont's extra season in between winter and spring.

Then, in the summer months, the rain travels down the hill of our driveway washing away little rivers of gravel and the puddles create potholes. The dirt then has to be pushed around to smooth it back out.

Why is all of this important? Because I lost my dime in February and found my dime in July. Between the plow, the dirt work and the rain, it doesn't seem possible that I would ever find my dime amidst all the moved dirt.

I believe Spirit sent my dime back to me to remind me of who I am and to write from my heart.

Here are the things I was reminded of when I found my dime.

1. Asking for help from Spirit works. I had asked for my dime to be returned for months. I didn't know why it was gone but I knew there would be a lesson for me.
2. In order to shine my light, I have to embrace being myself. When I do things to try to please others, it doesn't work. My writing flowed better when I did it my way instead of a prescriptive writing plan to impress a publisher.
3. Being grounded is important. Know where your feet are planted each and every moment. I can still see the dime in the dirt like it was a gift from Mother Earth. This work is continuous each and every day. It's important to not ruminate over the past or worry about the future. Be in the now.
4. Gratitude is an incredible gift to yourself. It truly changes how you think and it helps to raise your vibrational energy. Life is truly a miracle. We are meant to live each day with joy.
5. My emotions have a direct connection to the health of my physical body and how my life flows each day.
6. In order to heal, I had to feel healed within me. I took the supplements and did the treatments, but I believed my body was healing and this eventually became my reality.

I'm still learning to embrace who I am and live an authentic life; one where I turn to love instead of fear. A life where I believe in the possibility of an after-life right here on earth. A life where through sharing my journey, I am able to "help my peeps" and in return my peeps help me.

May you believe that coincidences truly are signs from the souls of our loved ones who left their physical bodies.

# 12

## Frames and Cars

"Decide. You are the only one in charge of your destiny. Unfair things may happen to you, unfortunate times may come to you, but you *always* get to choose how you respond. You can live in frustration and bitterness, or you can be the bigger person and just play the hell out of the cards you are dealt. Because the truth is in this world, not a single person chooses the cards they receive, but every single person chooses how to play them." ~Walk the Earth

"Livin' the dream!" has been my response throughout the pandemic whenever someone asks me, "How are you?" I've gotten many different reactions from people. "That's awesome!" to "I hear the sarcasm" to "Is it a nightmare?" When I recently said it after eating a delicious breakfast at our local diner, Lynn, the owner said, "I love it! That's what my shirt says!" Her smile was wide and I knew she meant it. There was no doubt in my mind that Lynn was truly embracing each day.

I first met Lynn in my twenties. I was a young mother about to have another baby. My mind wasn't worried about death and I hadn't developed my sincere gratitude for the many wonderful things in my life. I had severe back pain chasing around a toddler who never wanted to take a nap. To say I was exhausted was an understatement.

Lynn was quiet but kind and I was too busy to really be able to chat with her as I was swimming with my toddler and then racing home to get dinner on the table before falling on the couch, waiting for my next baby to come into this world.

I did have a sense of gratitude for this new baby because I had a miscarriage before this pregnancy. This caused me to worry during my entire pregnancy. The empty, hollow feeling I had when I lost my other baby still left a whole in my heart that may never be filled. A mother's love for a child is so monumental that those who have not felt it may never understand. Being connected to another human being who is growing inside of you is the best and most scary thing a person can live through. It's through the love that we experience such deep pain when we lose someone. I had experienced that and was extremely happy to be a Mom again to another human soul.

Years later Lynn would come back into my life and I watched her embrace each day with such gratitude and kindness. I thought about it some more and realized that none of us are promised a tomorrow. That's why right now is called the "present".

Nobody really knows exactly when death is going to happen but we all know that our time here on earth is limited. I know people who have been told they have months to live. Some died and others did not. That happened to Anita Moorjani. She was on death's door with cancer and she had a near death experience (NDE). The doctors told her family she wouldn't make it through the night. She entered another dimension during her illness, saw her beloved father and best friend in Heaven. Then she returned to her body and within five days the cancer was gone. She asked the doctors to stop all treatment. She knew she would be okay because she knew how to live her life now. Her book *Dying to Be Me* explains that her internal struggles were what were making her sick. She needed to be proud of who she was and embrace life. Now, she speaks and writes about being an empath and her NDE where she spontaneously healed her cancer, inspiring millions of people all over the world.

Lynn shared with me that she now has a journal in which she records her dimes because she has found so many since reading my first book.

Her excitement and sadness all rolled into one as she then shared her most recent dime story.

"I was so distraught. I had lost my other dog awhile back and now I wouldn't have any dogs left in the house. It was heartbreaking and I had difficulty even discussing it with anyone. I had a friend dig a hole where we were going to bury him. I went out to the hole to take a look and, there in the dirt, was a dime. It was in the middle of the field. I thought that was cool."

Her story went on like my dime stories- a continuous, never-ending collection of miracles.

"Then, when I went to the vet, I found a dime on the sidewalk. Finding each dime gave me a sense of peace and I really felt like my dog was right there with me. I would turn and even though my eyes didn't see anything, I knew he was there. I couldn't let go of the feeling. Then, you'll never believe this- I found another dime in my driveway when I got home. I seriously was like- okay, three dimes! My heart felt better and I still feel like he is right near my legs every time I walk into the house!"

Lynn glowed a happy light as she shared about her love for her dog and the connection to this invisible world.

We use frames to decorate and hang up pictures. The frame makes the picture look nice and it reminds us of a past moment to cherish. We never frame our worst moments in life. We try to capture the best moments like weddings, kids growing up or special places we visit. The truth is not all moments are picture perfect and would fit in a frame. We also frame our stories about how we view events in our life and this is based on our past experiences, which gives a different perspective for every event. Each event is different for the people experiencing it because they take in the experience based on their perspective.

How we choose to frame our stories is so important, especially when we are dealing with grief. This doesn't mean that we bury our grief. We are able to move through it in whatever way it shows up. We are able to have no expectations about the experience and we don't need to "heal" or feel like there's an end goal post to reach. Each day is different and different emotions are going to show up. It's okay to value and honor your feelings. Emotions come and go and most likely they won't be easy.

When you frame the story in a way where you are willing to feel your loved ones nearby and the possibility of an after-life, it may change your life forever. Framing your grief in a way that honors the past and begins to create more memories with those still here is a way to move through the new experiences without your loved ones.

Recently I was reading a post on social media. This mother lost her daughter to suicide. She wrote about crying when she looked at the laundry basket. She had used the basket many times since her daughter's death, but on this particular day, it seemed to bring up sadness. Maybe it was the extreme love for her daughter. She shared that she wasn't sure why she cried. Later on that day, she was able to laugh about the moment. Her story frame might have been I am going to allow myself to cry over this laundry basket and allow myself time to grieve. Then, she was able to look back at her grief, and take a moment to laugh.

Another woman, who had just lost her mother, shared another story about grief. She wrote, "Grief is a strange companion. At any moment an overwhelming sadness can creep up from behind to take you down unawares. Something seen or something thought. Which, it doesn't matter. After a while, it becomes expected. And, you cautiously sit and wait for it. As if you can best it. But wholly unexpected is the hilarity. Such as when my sister texts me from her walk telling me she can now "step on the sidewalk cracks". And I laugh. I even laugh a little too much. As if it's the funniest thing I've ever heard. But, there is this benefit after all, cracks" ~Angela Ogle

It's impossible to know and understand just how our minds work with memories. Every single time I pick up a spoon out of my drawer, I am reminded of our neighbor, Samantha. She transitioned so young. To everyone else, it might not make sense, but to me the memory rewinds in my head like a favorite song.

"This is the prettiest spoon I have ever seen in my life. Look at how beautiful this is! It is my favorite spoon and I like to use it each and every time I need a spoon," Samantha's happy go lucky voice was so incredibly excited over a simple spoon. As she showed me the spoon, I realized that it was from my silverware collection. I wish I could go back to that moment. I would have said this, "I'm so happy you like that spoon. It is one of my spoons but please keep it because it brings you such joy! I'm so happy to see you happy. If a spoon can do that, then you have at it!"

I didn't do that. Instead I laughed as I told her, "That is from my house." When I did that, Samantha felt that it belonged to me and gave it back to me. Looking back, she had such joy for that one spoon. Instead of beating myself up about it now, every time I pick up a spoon, I glory in the beauty of this particular spoon. Who would ever guess that every time I pick up that spoon I am reminded that life is sometimes cut short for some. Every time I pick up that spoon, I think of Sam and her family. They miss her bubbly energy each and every day.

Lynn's frame for her story includes "Livin' the Dream" because she is.

I like to compare life to driving a car. This analogy helps me frame my stories in a way where I am able to let go and enjoy life a bit more.

When I am driving a car, I feel like I have control and my anxiety is a bit less. Although I am able to control where the car is going, I can't control the other people driving near me. When someone else is driving, my anxiety kicks in because I feel like I don't have control over everything. I can't control where we go and I can't control what happens if another car comes near. I want to be able to stop the car or slow down if I think the person is going too fast.

Learning to live where we are working with the invisible divine energy and quantum physics requires us to drive our car (our life), but also to let go of the steering wheel once in a while. I used to drive with a tight grip and wanted control each and every day. Now, I choose the path to drive but allow the universe to guide me in a different way to my destination. When I grip so tight to the steering wheel, I get caught up in trying to control each and every part of my day. I have expectations for myself and others. I get caught up in being busy. This is how I spent most of my life. I thought the only way to live was to do, do, do and make sure I was in control of as many things as possible.

When I wrote my first book, I began to let go of the steering wheel. It was a slow process of learning to trust that the universe was helping me drive my car. It was sort of like when Hannah asked for a sign from her sister and allowed the most unexpected events to occur. When I let go, I choose the direction I want to go in life (writing, sharing my stories), but I let go of the steering wheel to allow the universe to drive me down a path I might not even know or understand yet. Like Lynn, I am now living my dream in a very different way. It's because of the faith I had in the universe and the gratitude for all the good and bad in my life.

There are going to be bumps along our journey. That is a given. It is how we frame those events that decides how the rest of the ride goes.

**"Death takes the body. God takes the soul. Our mind holds the memories. Our heart keeps the love. Our faith lets us know we will meet again." ~Nishan Panwar**

During our human journey, it is okay to be both sad and happy. It is okay to be both anxious and hopeful. You can be angry and excited. You can be lonely and grateful. You can miss your loved one and feel like they are right beside you.

Lori's first message to me said, "I wish I could see spirits!" Well, she can but she just doesn't know how to yet.

Lori lost her husband soon after she read *Dimes from Heaven*. She read my book as her husband slowly slipped back to his Spirit form. She wrote to me after and said, "I really thank God that I read your book before." After his death, she sent me several messages about signs from her dear, sweet husband.

"I wanted to share with you what happened at Dennis' service. The priest raised his glass and said do this in memory of me. Total silence and outside a jake brake came on. It couldn't have been more perfect! I believe that Dennis was saying ' I'm okay.' "

Dennis was a truck driver and even though Lori missed him, she felt so much love in her heart at that moment, just knowing that she was able to connect with him in a way she may never have imagined before.

Her next share melted my heart because she was teaching the next generation (her grandchildren) that we really can connect to Heaven and remember the love we have for family and friends.

"Dennis and I would always take the grandkids for a walk and they love throwing rocks in the pond and this is the outlet on the other side. This picture is the first time we went for a walk without him."

In the picture, there was a perfectly shaped heart in the grass. It was her next share that would show the deep connection Dennis still had with his family..

"They miss their Papa so much. Ryker was praying the other night and asked his mom if it was okay to thank papa for the heart rocks he sends him. He is three years old!"

Lori knows how to connect with Heaven now and is teaching the next generation that it is okay to feel this connection and know that it is true. She and her family have found many dimes, hearts and trucks. They feel Dennis nearby but also feel their sadness. It was her intention and belief in this connection that allowed the coincidences to happen.

**"One day, you are going to hug your last hug, kiss your last kiss, and hear someone's voice for the last time, but you never know when the last time will be. Live every day as if it were the last time you will be with the person you love." ~Anonymous**

When we frame our stories or drive our car, there are important questions to ask ourselves.

- Will this matter tomorrow?
- Will this matter in five years?
- What if I died tomorrow?

Framing the story with these questions may help put each event into perspective and allow you to let go of the steering wheel a bit to enjoy the ride. It's our memories that fill our hearts with love. We keep the old and create new at the same time.

Grief is not about letting go of those memories. It's about honoring those memories and connecting to those we love in Spirit form. When I think about my Grandmother and the memories inside of me, I feel such love surround me. Because of his Grandmother, Ryker is always able to feel his Papa's love in his heart.

When I visit my own grandchildren, I imagine my grandmother and bring that love with me. As each generation grows and then dies, we pass on this gift. I hope my own children and grandchildren always feel my unconditional love. It's the same love that we are able to receive from the universe or God or the Divine or whatever you want to call it.

I was so grateful when my friend, Ellen, sent me a dime bracelet. Immediately, I looked at the year as I believe that usually holds a clue as to the message from Heaven. It was the year my Grandmother passed away-1997. Instantly, I felt her presence and love.

I started writing because I was in physical pain. If it wasn't for the pain, I never would have started my new career as an author, Reiki Master and spiritual/intuitive coach and Angel card reader. I had no idea where this road would lead me all those years ago. I am thankful that I started this journey, and let go of the steering wheel a bit. Now I am able to connect with the Divine guidance that is available to every-one. When we are willing to acknowledge our pain by moving through it, this life may lead us to destinations we never could have imagined.

Most of my life, I have been a person who is always cold. Anything below seventy degrees and I would be bundled up like I was ready for a trip up Mt. Everest. Well, I may be exaggerating a bit, but this is important knowledge to show the point that when a friend shared that she was taking "cold" showers, my response was, "Good luck with that. I would never, ever do that." I could seriously not even understand why someone would ever want to take a cold shower. Then I learned more about body regulation and cold therapy, including the Wim Hof method. I got curious to see why anyone would do something that seemed so outrageous to me.

Cold showers help with the following: make you more alert, help you breathe deeper-increasing the oxygen level in your body, increases your white blood cell count (which increases your immunity to fight off diseases!), strengthens your will power and helps you maintain a healthy body weight. I never even had a clue about any of this.

Once I learned about it, it made more sense why a person might want to take a cold shower. First, you might take a hot shower. Then, you turn the water to cold and slowly adjust your body to the new temperature. You can put your arms and legs under the water and then move on to the rest of your body.

Cold showers changed my life. They taught me that I needed to learn more about something before I made a judgment about it. Sometimes my frames were wrong- the stories I had told myself for years were being reframed into something different. They taught me that I didn't really understand the why and how until I tried it myself. They taught me that I needed to connect my mind to my body. They taught me the answers I seek are actually within me.

My childhood version of Heaven was like my vision of a cold shower. I wasn't exposed to signs from Heaven so I didn't really understand. Now that I've experimented, just like the cold shower, I have come to understand more about how energy works and our connection to all souls.

The more that I connected to this lifestyle, the more I was able to access it and create a new reality. Our thoughts, both good and bad, are so powerful and once you realize this, you'll begin to see, hear, smell and feel differently than ever before.

Lynn shared with me recently that she finds dimes all the time now. She said that she checks the year and just asks what the message is for the dime. Sometimes it takes her a few days and then all of a sudden she has this thought. She said it feels like it is the right meaning and is glad she solved her own puzzle. Then she said, "I don't know if I am just making it all up or not, but whatever! I don't even know where these thoughts come from. It has meaning to me and that's good enough for me." Lynn is listening to and trusting her intuition and I am so happy for her. I'm glad that my books opened up this door for her.

Another time that I stopped into the diner, one of Lynn's waitresses wanted to give me a dime that she had received as a tip. It wasn't a usual dime. It was a gold dime. Abby explained that she found it in a weird spot. She had a tip with a bunch of change on a table that she was clearing. When she lifted up the salt and pepper holder, the dime was under that. Immediately, I knew that this dime was not actually meant for me. I felt a very strong intuitive sense that this dime was from Abby's grandfather, who had recently passed away. She still wanted me to have it but I knew the only way she was able to get the message was to share it with me. She was overwhelmed with love and her smile showed me she knew her grandfather would always be with her.

When I went for breakfast a few weeks later, Lynn spotted me at the table. She went behind the counter, grabbed something and came back to me. She shared that she recently found a dime in an unusual spot. She went to pick it up and it was tucked into a button. When she turned over the button, it said, "Never Let the Assholes Ruin Your Day".

My first two blog posts were about being grateful for garbage and toilet paper. If you had told me five years ago that I would be writing about these topics, I would have laughed. Who is grateful for garbage? I wasn't grateful for much of anything. I was living the American dream-house, family and job, but I wasn't really living each day with awe and wonder. It was through my experiences with grief and loss that I learned to look at life through a different frame and learn to drive my car in a very different way.

The universe likes to have fun with me now. I wrote a blog post about "Why I buy Toilet Paper in Bulk" in January 2020, two months before the nationwide shortage of toilet paper because people decided that if they had to be home, the one big thing they would need was toilet paper. When I set out to write, I had no idea the impact I might have on other people. Did my thoughts create this toilet paper coincidence? I'll never know but I knew inside that the universe was telling me to keep writing because I may be able to help others with my ideas. The coincidence was like a huge billboard sign flashing to me saying, "keep sharing!"

When I was first learning to drive, I remember my mother telling me that wearing mittens while I drove was dangerous. I could lose my grip on the steering wheel and that might cause an accident. She wanted me to wear gloves so that my hands wouldn't slip. I liked mittens better because they kept my hands warmer than gloves did. I recently bought these new mittens and went to drive my car. I could literally hear my mother's voice reprimanding me for wearing mittens. I also thought of the analogy of "driving safe." Yes, I wanted to be safe in this life, but I also want to let go of controlling each and every part of my life.

# Receiving More Keys to the After-Life

"I change my life when I change my thinking. I am Light. I am Spirit. I am a wonderful, capable being. And it is time for me to acknowledge that I create my own reality with my thoughts. If I want to change my reality, then it is time for me to change my mind." ~Louise L. Hay

**Education (about the Spirit world) + Intuition (using your natural born abilities) + Invisible energy= transformation,** the keys to understanding how our thoughts create our life.

Living a spiritual life is a journey that only some dare to travel. Some never do. It is a sweet dance between heaven and earth. Too much earth and we are disconnected from our spiritual self. Too much heaven and we are not enjoying our human journey on earth.

Living a more spiritual life has to do with letting go of the need to control everything and learning to work with the universe in a very different way than what we may have thought. It's reprogramming our subconscious so that we allow good in our lives. It's releasing the pain and hurt that lives within us so that we are able to love more and hurt less. We realize that our human body is just the car we are traveling in during this lifetime and that our engine is our soul that continues on after our death.

Before I published my book *Dimes From Heaven,* I read it to my father's best friend, Eldon. His approval was almost as good as receiving an approval from my own father. Eldon was someone who would be honest and give me the feedback I needed even if it might challenge me.

Eldon transitioned to Spirit while I was working on this book. The last time I spoke with him was on his birthday and the heavy breathing signaled to me that heart disease was affecting his "engine". I thought he might be transitioning soon.

I was standing at the edge of the paved street when I stared at the woman in the black jeep. She had stopped and I thought she was stopping to let me cross the road to the small bakery in town. She was but then she asked me, "Do you know where Jamison Road is?" It was exactly an hour and a half after I learned that Eldon had transitioned.

I froze right there in the middle of the road. I had no idea where "Jamison" road was but the name she said was just too close to my father's name, James, for me to not recognize it as a sign. I wasn't looking for a sign but here was my father letting me know that he and Eldon were reunited in Heaven. I thanked God when a woman behind me said, "Yeah- I know where Jamison road is." I couldn't even speak and these people had no idea this seemingly simple coincidence asking for directions was actually a sign from my dead father.

Later that same day, as my niece asked the waiter what mixed drinks were available, the waiter said, "Well, we also have a Mr. Palmer." As all of us chuckled, I explained to the waiter that my Dad's name was Mr. Palmer and we all think he might be here with us right now. He understood and apologized to us for our loss. It has been almost eight years but I still feel my Dad close by, especially when these things happen.

After these two signs from my Dad on the day Eldon died, I decided to request a specific sign from Eldon. I thought about my writing and wondered if I am able to follow my own advice about how to request a sign. Do I really have the power within me to create my reality? With either a sign from Heaven or something else? Like the first step of my directions stated earlier in this book- "Think of something that directly connects you and your loved one. Be specific." What would I ask for that would help me connect with Eldon?

Years ago Eldon shared a story with me about meeting his wife in the 1950's. Her and her mother were stranded on main street because they had locked the keys in their car. Eldon, wanting to be the hero, suggested that since he had the same car maybe his key would work. Like magic, Eldon opened the door to their car which in turn opened the door to Joyce's heart.

Thinking about this key story helped me figure out what sign I should ask for. "Send me something to do with a key please. I'm not sure if it is actually going to be a key but please send me a sign that involves a key of some sort. Thank you! Thank you! Thank you!" I thought about this in my head and didn't tell a single soul.

I let go and let God. I was super aware of everything in my environment. I was looking at my life like I was watching a movie. I felt like I was testing the universe. Was this what people mean when they talk about the power of quantum physics or manifesting? Can we really tap into this creative force of the universe to create a life filled with love? Do we have to feel the light within us for it to work? Do we need to change our energy inside of us to tap into this invisible field of energy? Am I really able to "order" what I want just like ordering a shirt or sweater on the internet?

This isn't like a child asking for a new toy for Christmas. It's such a deeper feeling from within, like the love I felt when I found the dime on top of the mountain.

The next day, nothing happened. I felt like Hannah must have felt when she didn't receive the sign from her sister. I mean, does this really work?

As I slammed the drawer of the antique wooden desk, I heard the clink on the floor and wondered if my Great Grandfather's spectacles, which were carefully placed on top of the desk, had fallen. I looked around and then spotted the guilty party. As I picked up the metal ornamental decoration that came unglued from the drawer, I looked deep into the keyhole and said, "Got it Eldon!" I had requested "something to do with a key" so this was good enough for me!

I felt shivers inside me like bubbles rising up in a fish tank as I stood alone in my house. I believed this was the sign I had requested and I didn't need anyone else to believe. I had created an event that was a message from Heaven with only my thoughts.

I went to bed a little earlier than usual that night. Still thinking about the sign from Eldon, I wondered if any more keys would appear.

It wasn't until the last sentence of the chapter that I realized Eldon was still going to help with that he used to call "God Moments"- which he had many throughout his life. I was reading the book *If I Die Before I Wake* by Eli Shaw. Eli's book was about the many ways he cared for people throughout his life. I was thinking of Eldon as I read this book because I remember him telling me that it would be difficult to take care of my father full time. He told me that I would get burned out being a full time care-giver. As caregivers, we forget to take care of ourselves. We get too busy with the needs of others.

He was right but I also treasured every moment that I was able to spend with my dad during his last days on earth. It was this burnout that caused me to ask for help. I couldn't work full time and care for my father. We were lucky to be able to hire full time around the clock care for my father. I transitioned from full time care seven days a week to monitoring my Dad's care through visits and periodic overnights with him.

I had been slow to read this particular book. Most books I whiz through and can read up to three or four books in a week. Looking back now, I see the reason for the timing of this particular chapter on this particular night. Eli shared about enjoying a sunset and slowing life down while caretaking for his friend who was dying. He compares life to a garden where everything is as beautiful as that sunset they watched that night. Gratitude became a way of life when he was faced with the upcoming expected death of a loved one.

Eli explains more about gratitude for all the things throughout the day. The miracle of the sun rising and setting each day. The glorious things like fresh water or coffee or the comfortable bed we sleep in. He compared life to a garden. What do we want in our garden of life? Do we want to take care of others? Do we want to paint or teach? What is it that we want in our garden? It's up to us to open the gate to our garden of life. First, we need to find the key to open the gate to our garden.

"I hope you find your key," was the very last sentence of the chapter. It didn't hit me until the last sentence that I was reading all about a key to life! I felt like a brand new door was opening and, just like the dime on the mountain, Eldon was showing me how "God Moments" would appear in my life. Eldon shared many God moments with me where the coincidence was so incredible that it helped solidify his faith, knowing that God was helping. Little did I know, Eldon was just beginning to play the key game like the dime game my dad liked to play. I can hear them laughing now as they plan each event over the next few weeks!

When I was a child, Eldon's family and my family went on many vacations to Florida where we always went to Disney World. The memories of walking into a restaurant and the look of shock when we told the hostess we needed a table for thirteen people still stays with me today. We had four kids in our family and Eldon had five kids. We were a wild, fun bunch.

As I walked down to the beach from the hotel, I saw a young boy getting his sandy feet washed off by his mom.

"I found a treasure!" he said to me as I peeked at the gold coins in his purple pail.

"Wow! Good for you!" I responded as I stepped down the next stair. "And, I found the key to Mickey Mouse's house!" he said. Was it just me or did this little boy just emphasize the word found and the word key? Was this random or was this heaven talking to me? I smiled as his mother explained that they are going to Disney tomorrow.

This woman and child have no idea what just happened. I know deep within me that Eldon was proving the magic of connecting to heaven, yet again, when I least expected it. I had decided the what- a key and Spirit decided the when and how!

I continued my walk toward the beach to catch up to my husband and babbled on about Eldon sending me another key. He smiled and knew how much this simple event meant to me.

As we walked near the ocean waves, I began to wonder about where life is leading me next. I'm close to retirement from my job in education but not exactly retirement age. I want to change my career and write full time, enjoy being a Reiki Master along with my coaching and intuitive angel card readings. How will I know if this is the right path to take? Was this book my key?

We walked and started talking about our newest Grandbaby who will be arriving soon. We have two sons and their sons will both have July birthdays too! We feel blessed to have four Morrissey boys all celebrating their birth within five days of each other!

I see the name "James" written in the sand and, I kid you not, the word "dad" right above it. Again, another crazy coincidence that happened just when I needed some reassurance and when I wasn't expecting it.

Just when we were about to turn around to walk back to the hotel, the most surprising sign gave me the answer I was searching for earlier, What do I do for this next part of my life?

There, written in the sand are the words, *"Once Upon a Time I helped my peeps."* I knew the title of this book was Once Upon a Dime and the theme was helping others understand how to use the communication system with our loved ones in Heaven and live in a more spiritual way. Death was again teaching me to live a very different life than I ever imagined. Writing was not a part of my life plan but here I was doing just that.

The next day before we left to fly home from Florida, I sat on the beach for as long as I possibly could. I wanted to absorb as much vitamin D as possible, listen to the ocean and sit in the sand. As I packed up my book and towel, I felt refreshed and ready to enjoy the day.

Dimes and keys also now show up in movies, in books and when people are talking to me. I don't necessarily always find an actual dime or key now. So, when I got into the elevator, I was shocked when the gentleman spoke the words three times like Dorothy in the Wizard of Oz clicking her shoes three times to take her home.

"Just when you think you have packed everything you need for your vacation but then realize you forgot something. You go to the store and you just can't believe how much they charge you for something. They just seem to nickel and dime you, nickel and dime you, nickel and dime you." Seriously, he had to repeat it three times? Well, honestly, had he not I might not have taken the sign as a message.

The key to my garden is writing and sharing my dime stories. I hope it helps my peeps to live a more spiritual life where we are connected to a universal energy where we know and understand how precious life truly is and that Heaven is right here with us each and every day.

When I first started writing about my grief, I had no idea where I was headed. Looking back now, I see how much I have learned about life through the lens of death.

Since our souls never die, when we leave our physical body, the soul is still communicating with those left behind. The energy of the person is always with us. We can tap into this with our thoughts- just like I did with the keys.

It was a quick hello but little did I know it would be a goodbye, the last time we ever would be able to communicate the way all humans know how- by being physically present. We almost ran into each other at the end of the grocery aisle. She was in a hurry and so was I- a reflection of how I was letting life pass by without appreciating my life. Forever, this memory of seeing Samantha helps me remember that tomorrow is never promised- a saying that is common but not really embraced for what it truly means. The very next day, Sam didn't wake up. I would never see her again. Now, whenever I see people, I always make sure to appreciate the moment and I play a little game when I go to the store.

I am always curious about how God is able to create such coincidences to help us learn during this lifetime. When I go to the store now, I ask myself, "Who am I going to see today?" It helps me imagine that God is supporting me. When I see people, I stop to chat and at least say hi. I appreciate that they were brought into my life. One time, on my way to the store, I happened to think of someone and wondered how her children were doing. Seriously, when I got to the store, she was there! Did I manifest seeing her? Or, was my intuition guiding me to the energy of this person? I'll never know but it was very interesting to have this experience.

I believed there was a way to communicate with those who had transitioned to Spirit, but I had no idea that this invisible communication system was so much bigger than just messages from our loved ones in Spirit. There is an invisible way to communicate and it is important to remember that our thoughts affect our external world.

I began applying this invisible communication system to other areas of my life and I realized that the message my mind sent to my body affected my health. I realized that I sent messages to other people using energy instead of words. It was these thoughts that would determine my inner and outer world.

My father thought his body was like a car he could fix. As a mechanic, he solved all types of car engine difficulties. It was his life's work. He thought the doctors were mechanics of the body. You might have a leaking engine. Let's fix it! What he didn't understand was that his body was carrying his soul and, if he lost control of listening to his soul, it wouldn't matter what a doctor could do.

Our bodies respond to our thoughts in both positive and negative ways. I have no idea what my father's thoughts were that affected his heart so much so that he spent thirty three years fighting heart disease. I know he must have been stressed out owning his own business and providing for his family. My Dad believed in the doctor's superpowers but our bodies aren't like cars that can be easily fixed with a mechanic or doctor.

Since the heart represents love, security and joy, I am able to see how my father's love for his family made him want to work hard to provide financial security for all of us. When he did this, he may have lost his sense of joy.

He worked hard, ate Snickers bars for lunch and lived on cortisol in his veins like bad oil in a car engine. Even with his smiles and his sense of humor, his body couldn't hold up. When I was about to make a change in my career, I thought a lot about my dad's fight for survival. I myself had been in a cortisol storm for the past ten years and my cholesterol level showed it. The stress was getting to me and my soul wanted me to listen. I was juggling a lot at work and knew that in order to enjoy my life, I had to make some big changes.

I used to live my life in the thought pattern of "I'll be happy when...." Here are a few of my favorites over my lifetime:

- I'll be happy when I get married.
- I'll be happy when I have a baby.
- I'll be happy when I get a teaching job.
- I'll be happy when I get a different job.
- I'll be happy when I move out of my house.
- I'll be happy when I receive a sign from my friend, mother, father, grandmother, daughter, son or whoever I am missing.
- I'll be happy...well, you get the idea, right?

My happiness was based on the "next best thing in my life." I was always chasing happiness. It wasn't yet a part of my daily life.

Now, I've stopped thinking that I'll be happy when....I'm happy right now. My gratitudes each and every day are many. I'm happy writing and sharing my story with all who want to read it and I'm grateful and blessed for each day that I am alive. Life is too short to keep chasing happiness. We truly never know how much time we all have here and I've decided that I am going to be at peace with whatever happens in my life.

I asked Spirit for help and was amazed when the messages were clear. My father came to me in a dream and said, "Don't make the same mistake I made. If I could go back, I'd do it all differently. I wouldn't work so much and I wouldn't have stressed out so much. I realize now that by stressing myself with my thoughts, it affected my body in ways that were invisible. These invisible worries created chaos inside my body and then eventually showed up in the form of heart attacks."

My Dad was forty-six when he almost died of a heart attack. I was turning fifty-four this year and with my cholesterol over two hundred fifty, it was time for me to listen to his guidance. I used what I knew about asking for signs from the other side to help guide me in my life.

Here are the adapted directions to change your thoughts from worry to something positive.

Step 1: Think of something that you are worried about. Be specific

Step 2: Write down why this worries you.

Step 3: Change the belief to something positive and believe it has already happened.

Step 4: Ask and allow the universe and your spirit guides to support you and help you with a positive outcome.

Example

1. I'm worried about selling my house.
2. I'm worried that it is not the right decision.
3. I sold my house and all is well. I have the resources to be able to move forward in my life.
4. I am grateful for my Spirit Guides supporting me during this transition in my life.

This connection to something bigger and the invisible communication system wasn't something that I could see. I needed to tap into this in order to create the life I wanted- one filled with love, peace, forgiveness and joy. At first, it was like a game I was trying to learn how to play.

The trick is that it's not only what we think about but how our bodies are feeling. We are vibrational, energetic beings meant to live joyful lives. We are meant to experience Heaven on Earth during our time here. Instead (myself included), we have gotten caught up in the stress of what society, our ancestors and our linear brains told us we were here for. We get stressed out with our jobs and that affects our energy.

Some religions dictate that our behavior is going to determine whether we go to Heaven- putting pressure on perfectionism and sets in motion the negative voice of worry.

Some schools send the message that we aren't good enough unless we go to college and get a high paying job.

Some of us try to make our parents proud by trying to meet the unwritten expectations parents place on us.

Some of us get so caught up in our mistakes that we can't seem to move forward in our lives.

I have a whole new perspective of life and death. When I step back from all of the demands placed on us and the beliefs that society has told us, what is there?

There is love.

There is peace.

There is joy.

If I was to write advice to my Younger Me, here is what I would tell her:

- Life is a gift and tomorrow is seriously not promised. Our life could end at any time. Enjoy each day so if something happened to you or someone else, you would have no regrets.
- Love your body and stop worrying. Appreciate every part of your body because your body needs to know that you love it.
- See others' souls and love them because if you love yourself, then you have the ability to love and accept others.

- Listen to your body and take care of it. You only get one and it's important to make it last a long, long time!
- Nature resets your natural body rhythm. No matter what, get outside each day for at least 20-30 minutes. An hour is even better.
- Remember the legacy of the people who have passed and embrace that core value that they were able to give you. Think of it as a gift from their spirit.
- Appreciating abundance is okay to do.
- Being confident is a good thing.
- Stop comparing yourself to others.
- There is enough and more for everyone. Abundance comes from within and believing that you deserve greatness.
- Notice how your brain tries to keep you safe by telling you lies- it automatically turns to fear. Tell it to shut up and feel love within yourself.
- Feel soul connection with yourself first and then with others.
- We are all one in an ocean of love.

**"Just as harnessing electricity changed the outer world, when we learn how to harness the true power and intelligence of the heart, everything will change about how we think and feel, and how we relate to one another." ~ Heart Math Institute**

I have a necklace with two hearts on it. Recently, my grandson said, "Grandma, you have two hearts on your necklace!" He was in the moment and noticed something so simple yet so wonderful. I felt and thought, "Yes, darling. They are your heart and my heart connected. You are loved." I try to feel the connection to everyone around me with this necklace. It helps me turn to love instead of fear.

My friend, Carrie, shared recently that she finds four-leaf clovers all the time now. She often finds them while walking her grandson on the road that I live on. I am so happy to see her spending time with her grandson and that she is aware and looking for miracles. When we begin to look for small miracles, oftentimes we begin to feel so incredibly grateful for our lives. She treasures her time with her grandson and knows that the four leaf clovers are most likely a sign from her loved ones.

I experienced asking and receiving something recently that showed how we can use this practice to attract or manifest other things in our life. It wasn't a message from Spirit but I was able to mold my reality with my thoughts. I was organizing and cleaning my basement for weeks. The energy felt clean and fresh after I painted and vacuumed my new work from home office. I had new pine bookshelves, a beautiful wooden desk and my Grandmother's coffee table set up with a salt lamp and an essential oil diffuser. I was clearing out the clutter in my life and making space for new opportunities; both literally and figuratively.

At the same time, I started doing intuitive angel card readings as part of my health and life coaching business and it allowed me to release old fears about sharing my stories about the afterlife. The energy inside me was like a spring flower blossoming.

Soon after, an absurd idea popped into my head. As I was getting dressed after my massage, I noticed a spider plant on the coffee table at my massage therapist's office. Like a lonely cloud drifting across a clear blue sky, a thought blew into my mind that I seriously wanted a spider plant for my new office space. I remembered reading somewhere that a spider plant helps clean the air in a room. This idea was absurd because I have never been able to keep any household plant alive for more than a few weeks. I never knew which plants wanted more or less water, or whether or not they wanted more or less sunshine. It was almost like the plant could sense my stress. I had given up years ago on having any plants inside my house.

Once, my sister gave me a plant that was from my great grandparents' house. She didn't understand that there was no way this plant would survive when entrusted to my care. Sure enough, months later I gave her back the yellow ceramic pot filled with what looked like only dirt and no sign of any plant life. Luckily, my niece was able to bring it back to life. Because I almost killed that plant, it was ludicrous that this idea of a spider plant popped into my mind.

Then this stronger feeling came through. It was persistent. "No, I really, really, really want a spider plant." The thought was no longer a cloud; it was like a magnet sticking to my mind. I tried to let the idea go again but since it wouldn't, I resolved it with the thought, "Well, if a spider plant appears in my life, maybe I'll try again."

I forgot all about the silly idea about a spider plant and did not talk to anyone about it. I was technically "ordering" a spider plant from the universe, just like ordering a package from Amazon. I wasn't sure the how or the when but I had put the energy out that I would accept a spider plant for my new office, if one came along.

This is where the spirituality part of being human appears and surprises even those of us who know and understand how the universe works. Other people are able to hear our thoughts even without being connected by a telephone or even speaking the words. It can sometimes creep people out if you have ever had this happen. Have you ever thought of someone and then they text or call you? This way of communication seems so unbelievable at times but it is most definitely real.

In a town about forty-five minutes away, at about the time I was thinking those thoughts, one of my Southern New Hampshire University students was preparing to mail a thank you card to me. He not only mailed me that card, but he carefully placed something inside the card.

I had "ordered" a spider plant and I received it in Neil's thank you card! I was so shocked that it took me two days to reach out to Neil to share this crazy coincidence.

Neil read my book and was inspired by my story. He was an educator and understood how our thoughts create our reality. It wasn't always something we were able to talk about when working in public education. My story changed his life and he was changing mine. He was proof that universal intelligence or God or whatever this energy was could hear our thoughts and respond to create our reality. This is true for receiving signs from Spirit but can also be applied to other areas in our life. That's why it's important to filter your thoughts because what you think may come true. What appears in your life is exactly what you think about.

Think negative thoughts and more negativity appears in your life. Think positive thoughts and more positive things appear in your life. My daily gratitude practice includes starting and ending my day with being thankful. I begin each day with ten or eleven gratitudes. I write in a notebook and add an explanation as to why I am grateful. Some examples are "I am grateful for my morning cup of coffee because I love the taste of coffee and it wakes me up." or "I am grateful for my house because it is a wonderful place to live." At the end of the day, I hold a rose quartz rock to my heart and think of the one best thing that happened during my day. This trains my brain to remember all of the good things. From driving home from work safely or watching the sun set or dinner with family, I always find several things I am grateful for.

Grief is inside each and every one of us. It sits like a rain cloud ready to burst open at the mere memories that live in our minds. Whether we stuff it down or let it rise up, we are able to feel deep love within.

I was born in 1968. The telephone had been around for a while but at that time many would have thought the concepts on the Jetson's animated cartoon were make believe. Video calls and microwaves seemed like an impossible idea. It was only for the imagination. Nowadays, people Facetime easily and most homes have a microwave that creates invisible heat! We also store information on an invisible "i-cloud". Just because we can't see it, doesn't mean it doesn't work.

At a crossroads for understanding, there are now many scientists proving this idea of an invisible connection to what they term consciousness. They describe this consciousness continuing on after the physical body has died and there are many studies proving both Mediums and Psychic abilities for some people.

Liz Enton notes the scientific researchers in her new book, *WTF Just Happened*. Liz was very science minded but found comfort during her journey with grief by the verified studies completed by both The

Forever Family Foundation and the other scientists around the world. Now, Liz believes that there is a strong possibility that consciousness survives our bodily death.

If I had been five minutes later or earlier, I would have missed it. If I had not forgotten my purse in my husband's truck, I would have missed it. If my radio had been set to Sirius XM instead of the local radio station, I would have missed it. If I hadn't asked a friend to come thirty minutes later, I would have missed it. If I hadn't unpacked the groceries first, I would have missed it. If I hadn't taken part of the day off for a doctor's appointment, I would have missed it. The list could go on and on. The fact is: I didn't miss it and the title of this book was sent to me by Spirit because I let go of the steering wheel.

I let go and didn't worry about leaving my purse somewhere. I let go and didn't worry about asking my friend to come a little later. I let go and didn't worry about making another trip downtown. I let go and took care of myself by going to get the medicine to help me feel better. I let go of the day to go exactly how I planned it to go.

I had been thinking about the title of my book all day. I was meeting with someone about my book and I couldn't figure it out. I had a list about a page long and had asked a few friends what they thought of all of the different possible titles.

"Kim, would you mind coming at 1:30 instead of 1:00? I need to run to the store and get some medication before we meet about my book."

"Of course. I'll see you at 1:30," Kim graciously agreed.

I felt bad. I hate being late and I hate not showing up to something I had agreed to prior. I was asking for something that I needed, which was so hard for me. Why do I struggle asking for something so simple? I know the answer. I have spent most of my life caring for everyone else instead of myself. My frame was to take care of others before I took care of myself- something I had done my whole life to try to make others happy.

I needed the medication to help me feel better and because I had forgotten my purse in my husband's truck, I had to come home to get an extra insurance card. That meant I had to make an extra trip back downtown.

"Come on down to our Once Upon a Dime sale. Live Happily Ever After in a Nicer, Newer Car for just one dime down!" The Shelburne Mitsubishi ad on the local radio show came on the radio as soon as I started my car.

"Thank you Dad," was all I thought as I was dreaming of a life happily ever after where I live in a more spiritual, connected way. I hope *Once Upon a Dime* helps you to connect to your intuition, your natural born gifts and that you are able to feel your loved ones right beside you.

**"One day she woke up different. Done with who was with her, who was against her, or walking down the middle because they didn't have the guts to decide. She was done with anything that didn't bring her peace. She realized that opinions were a dime a dozen, that validation was for parking, and loyalty wasn't a word, but a lifestyle. It was this day that her life changed. And not because of a man, or a job, but because she realized that life is way too short to leave the key to your happiness in someone else's pocket."**
**~Anonymous**

While looking up to see who wrote this quote, I found the quote on a site that said, **"Relationship Rules. A Safe Haven for emotional human beings."**

You have everything you need within you and your loved ones keep showing you they are still here with you. Believe in this connection.

The keys to life are always inside me like my keys to my car being in my pocket.

When I walk away from my car with the keys in my pocket, my car beeps. I imagine my father and Eldon telling me,

**"The answers are within you. Take your keys wherever you travel. Notice the signs. Believe in more. Get rid of outdated subconscious belief systems that no longer serve you. Connect to your intuition and know that we are always with you."**

Heaven is trying to get our attention through dreams and synchronicities. Now, you know how to listen.

CPSIA information can be obtained
at www.ICGtesting.com
Printed in the USA
BVHW052007160623
666068BV00004B/87